THE BIG IDEA
WHEN GOD IMPREGNATES YOUR IMAGINATION

BY

DR. JAMAL H. BRYANT

WITH

DENNIS J. WOODS

LIFE TO LEGACY, LLC

From Hattie - To Julia - 2015

Printed in the United States

10 9 8 7 6 5 4 3 2 1

Library of Congress Control Number: 2014956313

Published by
Life To Legacy, LLC
P.O.Box 57
Blue Island,
60406
www.Life2Legacy.com

Contents

INTRODUCTION

Ironically, big ideas can come in all shapes and sizes. Whether it's the latest idea that will revolutionize a particular industry or a better way to complete mundane day-to-day tasks at home, the right idea at the right time is a powerful combination for success. Look around you today, everyone seems to be talking about success and making it "big." Everyone wants to reach super-sized status whether it is in their homes, businesses, or even churches, people want to do it big.

Society's fixation with big success and striking it rich can be seen throughout the country. By the millions, people stand in line for their chance to pick the winning lottery number or flock in droves to gambling casinos in hopes of making it big. However, I would submit to you that they are looking for that "big break" or a "big idea" in all the wrong places.

One of the most popular prime-time shows on television today is *Shark Tank*. On this program, successful multi-millionaires and billionaires listen to hopeful entrepreneurs pitch their "big ideas" to get the sharks to invest in their business ventures. Since the show has been airing, hundreds of would-be successful entrepreneurs have stood before this panel of tenacious money moguls. However, that doesn't compare with the countless millions of people that tune in every week to see whose "big idea" will get capitalized next. The fact that this show has garnered so much popularity speaks to the reality that there are many more people watching this program, who imagine themselves in the spotlight pitching their life-transforming "big idea." They say, "if I could only come up with the next big idea, I could be a success too."

However, big ideas do not happen by osmosis or occur in a vacuum. For the believer, they are intricately tied to our covenantal relationship with God and our divine destiny. Our God is big and similarly, every idea that He has is pregnant with immeasurable wealth in both the natural and spiritual realms. Whenever God gives you an idea, it is a big idea because it came from a big God.

There are two passages of scripture that will help you grasp the concept of the big idea. The first one is found in Deuteronomy 8:18, where the Lord declares, "But thou shalt remember the LORD thy God: for *it is* he that giveth thee power to get wealth, that he may establish his covenant..." (KJV). As it states in this passage, it is God that gives us the power *to get* wealth not to *create* wealth. God has already created all the wealth. All the silver and gold belongs to him, as does the cattle on a thousand hills. He brings forth bread from the ground by providing the wheat. All the wealth that is in the earth realm, God put it there, and it is He who gives to us the ability and the "ideas" on how to get it. For example, oil is just a thick greasy liquid-like substance, until you come up with a big idea on how to refine and use it. Once people learned how to use petroleum, it produced a great deal of wealth.

The second scripture is Joshua 1:8 which reads:

This book of the law shall not depart out of thy mouth; but thou shalt meditate therein day and night, that thou mayest observe to do according to all that is written therein: for then thou shalt make thy way prosperous, and then thou shalt have good success. (KJV)

In other words, when you meditate on God's precepts, His life-giving word impregnates your imagination and dreams with big ideas and seeds of destiny that can transform every area of your life. Not all success is good. Good success is more than money in the bank. Good success is a dynamic relationship with God, a fruitful relationship with others, health and prosperity, blessings in all of your ways, and the desire to fulfill God's purpose for your life.

Sadly, so many people are rich in material wealth but poor towards God. In St. Matthew 16:26 Jesus asked, "What good will it be for someone to gain the whole world, yet forfeit their soul? Or what can anyone give in exchange for their soul?" However, one person armed with a big idea from an immeasurably big God can transform a family, a community, a nation, and the world, all for the glory of God.

Our God has such big plans for us that we cannot possibly comprehend it in our own ability. Therefore, he uses our imagination and dreams to take us beyond the confines of our normal way of thinking. He teaches us how to walk by faith and not by sight and how to trust Him in the face of overwhelming odds and adversity. God is not a respecter of persons. With

Him, all things are possible. Therefore, you do not need prestige, a college degree, or pedigree to be successful. All you need is a word from the Lord to impregnate your imagination and inspire you to achieve your God-given dreams.

One
IMAGINATION AND FAITH

O ne of today's sensational Gospel recording artists, Tamela Mann, released an anointed song entitled, *I Can Only Imagine*. In this chart-topping single, Tamela imagines what it would be like to be standing before the Lord in glory. Enraptured in ecstasy, she contemplates what her reaction would be when she finally beholds the Lord face-to-face. In the context of her imagination, she vacillates between being dumbfounded or breaking out in total praise; between standing in adoration or falling down to her knees. Surrounded by all His glory, she wonders what would her heart feel. Would she dance there before Him, or in awe just stand still? Unable to resolve her ecstatic dilemma, she retreats to her place of wonderment by simply saying, "I can only imagine." The lyrics of this inspirational song give us a glimpse into the vital role that imagination plays in the life of a believer.

It was the incomparable genius Albert Einstein who stated, "Imagination is more important than knowledge. For knowledge is limited to all we now know and understand." From Einstein's quote and from the lives of historic biblical patriarchs and prophets like Abraham, Joseph, and Daniel, we can deduce that the impetus for human potential and achievement begins with imagination. From the wellspring of imagination, knowledge is acquired, volition is ignited, and achievement is actualized.

The *Dictionary of Psychology* defines imagination as "the reorganization of data derived from past experiences, with new relations, into present ideational experience." In other words, imagination is the ability to take past thoughts and ideas and blend them with new ones, creating a picture within your mind. Imagination is most utilized by children because they're oblivious to all of the stressors and complexities of life, and haven't been indoctrinated by tradition or boxed in by conformity. In Luke 18:17, Jesus states emphatically, "Truly I tell you, anyone who will not receive the kingdom of God like a little child will never enter it." From the Lord's admonishment, we must ask ourselves, what is it that adults can learn from a child? The answer is how to have an active imagination and faith without limits.

If you ask any child about what it is they believe their father can do, without reservation, they will tell you "my daddy can do anything." To a child, if daddy said it, that settles it, they believe it. A child's faith is not in competition with what is happening in the world around them. Children do not regard politics, one's race, ethnicity, or social-economic status. In a child's mind, none of those things has any place. Whatever momma or daddy tells them they take it at face value and do not concern themselves with any of the complexities of achieving it. They just process the parent's promises in an imaginative milieu of limitless possibility.

It is because of this very fact that Jesus said that having child-like faith is the template for kingdom advancement. Our faith ought not to limit us or box us in with a system of rules or societal norms. Instead, our faith should be radical enough to prevent us from conforming to fear, doubt, and limitations, even when we're challenged with the seemingly impossible. The simplicity in which a child processes their faith does not rely on what experience has taught them. Where a child has few life experiences to draw on, they compensate with imagination.

IMITATIVE AND CREATIVE IMAGINATION

There are two types of imagination. The first is *imitative* imagination. The second is *creative* imagination. Imitative imagination is simply the mind's reconstruction of the past. We use our memory to picture something we've experienced, and then we recreate it. Imitative imagination works best with children. When you see them playing doctor or playing teacher, they're remembering an encounter that they had, then interjecting themselves as the central character. You'll notice that when children play doctor, none of them volunteer to be the patient. They all want to be the doctor. That's because when you're engaging in imitative imagination, you want to be the principal character, not the supporting character. No one imagines himself or herself running in a race and coming in second place. Imitative imagination always puts you out front as the winner.

In a similar way, we should use imitative imagination to fuse ourselves into scripture. Take, for instance, the scripture where Jesus said to the disciples, "Greater things than these will you do." Imitative imagination won't allow you to think that Jesus was only referring to those disciples when He said "you." It will give your mind permission to realize that He was addressing you as well and that you have the ability to activate the same miraculous power Jesus had. Imitative imagination will cause you to declare, "I can see myself doing greater works." I implore you to conceptualize being more than a conqueror. I beseech you to conceptualize being that overcomer.

Unfortunately, too many of us have fallen into a spirit of apathy, accepting that we'll never do or become anything greater than what we've already done or become. However, I want to encourage you to believe that you can choose the ending of your story. When I was younger, I was fond of a series of books that fully engaged my imagination by allowing me to choose my own ending to the story. My question to you is whose report will you believe? Will you believe the report of the Lord, or will you choose an alternate ending plagiarized by the devil? Many of you have arrived at a juncture in life where God is affording you the opportunity to choose your own ending, based on the expansion or limitation of your imagination. The question is will you start seeing yourself as the victor or continue seeing yourself as the victim?

Let's now take a look at how the second dimension of imagination—*creative* imagination—works in our lives. Creative imagination is the restructuring of past sensory impressions. It involves mental imagery that relies on past experiences to construct a sensation that doesn't even exist. Seeing what the eyes have not seen, hearing what the ears have not heard—that's creative imagination. Creative imagination and faith have similar modus-operandi because neither depends on the actual or factual to operate.

In the King James Version of the Bible, Hebrews 11:1 gives us a working definition for faith, which is, "… the substance of things hoped for, the evidence of things not seen." To a logical person, the definition of faith doesn't make sense. This is why imagination is the perfect ingredient to activate faith. The key component of the biblical definition of faith is, "things hoped for." Things that are hoped for trigger your imagination. Then imagination produces the picture in your mind to keep that hope alive. Though the things hoped for don't currently exist, imagination bridges the gap between hope and manifestation, allowing you to operate as though the thing hoped for is already present. The (b) clause of Hebrews 11:1 in the Amplified Bible parenthetically states: "faith perceiving as real fact what is not revealed to the senses." It's for this very reason that faith and the scientific method can't coexist, because the latter depends on testing and proving the observable.

In the book *Natural Childhood* by John Thomson, he surmised "imagination in play provided the basis for [children] to grow up and eventually to live in the outside world [with flexibility]." Children who develop in an environment where it's safe to engage in active imagination aren't easily stifled later on in life because their imagination as a child gave them a passport to think outside the box. Once you migrate into the world of imagination, you develop a capacity for flexibility. People who are able to imagine will never get backed into a corner because they know how to think themselves out of it. They aren't just logical, linear, rational, 2-D (horizontal and vertical) thinkers. They're 3-D thinkers who conceptualize not just in terms of height and width, but in terms of depth as well. The 3-D thinking child is adept at seeing things in the creative and faith realms, but that's beyond the reach of the 2-D thinker.

Therefore, imagination never partners with logic. Imagination never sleeps with science. Imagination never flirts with facts. When you have imagination, you don't require an empirical basis. You can't be logical and operate in the faith dimension because faith never makes logical sense. Imagination doesn't require an endorsement by education but is inspired by desire. Consequently, having a Ph.D. doesn't give you an imagination. Having six figures in a bank account doesn't give you an imagination. But having a yearning on the inside of you that says, "Where I am is not where God wants me to be," will spark your imagination and trigger your desire.

Individuals who are destined for greatness learned early on as children to use imagination and ingenuity to compensate for lack. If they didn't have a drum set, they would make rhythmic beats on buckets, pails, and empty suitcases. If they didn't have a guitar, they would stand in front of a mirror strumming a broom and pretending to be a star. If they wanted to play cops and robbers, they would use a stick like a rifle and a hammer for a pistol. Therefore, imagination is at its maximum when you're forced to work with the minimum.

THE FAITH COMPONENT

The United Negro College Fund's motto, "A mind is a terrible thing to waste," is true because the mind is more than just the seat of personality, character, and knowledge. It's also the birthplace of imagination. For most of us, it's difficult to fathom a mind devoid of imagination. Truly, that would encompass the meaning of the phrase "a wasted mind." However, it's essential that we understand that the mind is more than just a place where information is stored, for information alone will not cause manifestation. For example, a computer contains billions of bytes of information and can make thousands of simultaneous computations per second, but it has no imagination. Therefore, a computer can't observe a great bald eagle soaring high in the sky, and then imagine itself being able to fly too. The computer doesn't have an imagination that could inspire it to overcome the challenges of engineering, master the laws of aerodynamics, and then conceptualize and build an A380 Airbus. Clearly, as Einstein espoused, imagination is more important than knowledge, for whatever is known as a fact, imagination preceded it.

In our examination of imagination, we must understand how imagination and faith work together. In Mark, chapter 9, an encounter with a man whose son was possessed by a demonic spirit will help us understand some of the dynamics and power akin to imagination. Our text reads:

> A man in the crowd answered, "Teacher, I brought you my
> son, who is possessed by a spirit that has robbed him of speech.
> Whenever it seizes him, it throws him to the ground. He foams

at the mouth, gnashes his teeth and becomes rigid. I asked your disciples to drive out the spirit, but they could not." So they brought him. When the spirit saw Jesus, it immediately threw the boy into a convulsion. He fell to the ground and rolled around, foaming at the mouth. Jesus asked the boy's father, "How long has he been like this?" "From childhood," he answered. "It has often thrown him into fire or water to kill him. But if you can do anything, take pity on us and help us." "'If you can'?" said Jesus. "Everything is possible for one who believes."

Mark 9:17-18, 20-23

Three components of this text are essential to this aspect of our study: the problem, the power to overcome the problem, and the imagination to access the desired result. The first element is the problem. In each case where Jesus performed a miracle, there was some lack or deficiency to overcome. In this case, there was a young lad possessed with a mute spirit. However, it is noteworthy that his speech wasn't the only thing that was impaired. This mute spirit also caused violent epileptic-type seizures and suicidal episodes.

The second element is the power to overcome the problem. There comes a time in everyone's life when parishioners or pastors won't be able to help you. That was the case with this desperate father who was trying to help his debilitated son. Jesus' disciples encountered the possessed young man first but were unable to exorcise the demonic spirit. They didn't have the power to change the problem. However, when Jesus stepped into the scenario, the dynamics of the dilemma changed. No matter how profound the problem, when Jesus is present, the impossible immediately shifts to the possible. Whenever you introduce Jesus into any circumstance, problem, lack, or deficiency, the power to change the problem is now present.

The third and final element is the faith and imagination to access the desired effect. One might ask, where the imagination element is found in this text. I submit to you that it's tacitly implied in what Jesus said to the boy's father. "Everything is possible for one who believes." What you and I believe will determine whether we will actualize manifestation in our circumstances. Notice that Jesus didn't say *this* thing is possible. He said *everything* is possible. With those words, Jesus took the lid off limitation because the potential of faith is limitless.

The reason why most of us don't see greater manifestation in our circumstances is because we place limits on our hopes and dreams. We simply cannot wrap our minds around the concept that *all things* are truly possible, because we have possessed too much disinformation that militates against our faith. To receive all things being possible, you need the imagination component of faith. That's the only way to grasp a concept that's beyond what's real now. That's why the Bible says that faith is the substance of things hoped for, and the evidence of things not seen. In that unseen realm of the Spirit, truly *everything* is possible.

The word *everything* refers to that which is limitless. *Everything* goes beyond the observable and the tangible. *Everything* supersedes logic and empirical evidence. *Everything* eliminates the limitations of the science and trumps the impact of political power and prestige. *Everything* includes the things not seen, and evidence for things that have not yet occurred. *Everything* demands having the faith to believe without hesitation or reser-

vation that God can do anything, no matter what the circumstances say. However, wrapping your mind around the possibility of everything requires imitative and creative imagination.
Though we serve a God that no man has seen at any time, like
Tamela Mann so melodically sings, "I can only imagine what
it would be like ...."

Two
MILITATING AGAINST IMAGINATION

Positive imagination is inspiring and empowering. However, we must also examine the effects that negative impressions have on imagination. Researchers in Sweden have discovered that our imagination can change our perception of reality. Our minds have the ability to manipulate messages by changing them to what we want to hear and see. The Karolinska Institutet's scientific journal has proven that the human brain combines information from different senses, and our imagination is a major contributor as to how our brain processes that information.

In that esteemed Swedish institution, a professor by the name of Henrik Ehrsson conducted a study where he proved what power imagination had on one's perception of reality. In this experiment, participants experienced the illusion of two passing objects. Just when the objects were passing each other, they interjected a sound as if they collided, but they had not.

By merely hearing the sound, the participants believed a collision occurred. Dr. Ehrsson claims his research proved that one's imagination is strong enough to alter our perception of reality, all due to sensory influence alone. The results of this experiment lend insight on how the brain often fails to distinguish between thought and reality. The imagination does not have the ability to separate between what is real and what is fantasy. We have all experienced this when watching a movie. Consciously, we know the movie is not real, only actors acting on a set. However, once our imagination is engaged through sensory influence, we can become emotional and cry, get angry, experience fear, joy or delight. At the point when that first tear drops, our brain is not distinguishing between reality and fantasy, but has fully engaged our emotions based on sensory influence. Whereas this inability works well in a movie theater, it can present serious difficulty for an individual who cannot control which thoughts they act upon. Whenever a person's brain is unable to separate between thought and reality, this condition meets a major criterion for the clinical diagnosis of schizophrenia.

If one doesn't have discipline over their imagination, they'll be unable to discern what's real and what's imagined. Have you ever witnessed a schizophrenic person walking down the street talking to himself? Surprisingly, it's not a one-way conversation. They're actually entertaining what psychiatrists and psychologists call *audio hallucinations*, which is symptomatic of those diagnosed with schizophrenia. The voices they hear aren't actually real but are subjectively real within the confines of their own psychosis. This type of imbalance is the basis for insanity.

However, as a Christian, in our normal course of living, we do things that the secular world around us would categorize as crazy. We walk by faith and not by sight, which means we have to be able to see what doesn't exist. For example, here is what Paul says in 2 Corinthians 4:18:

> So we don't look at the troubles we can see now; rather, we fix our gaze on things that cannot be seen. For the things we see now will soon be gone, but the things we cannot see will last forever. (NLT)

How are we to fix our gaze on things that can't be seen? We do it by faith! Hebrews 11:1 tells us that "faith is the substance of things hoped for, [and] the evidence of things not seen." You have to see what is not, in the presence of what is, yet not let those current circumstances that you want to come out of cause you to lose focus. You focus on the Lord and magnify Him for the things that are not yet in existence. Praise Him as though they were. Once you can grasp this spiritual truth, you'll realize that the only mental faculty preventing you from slipping into depression and acting out on suicidal ideations is your own imagination. Oftentimes, it's your imagination showing you that you're going to arrive at a better place.

From the Bible we learn that imagination, like faith, is so substantive that God can judge you based off of it alone. In Matthew 5:28, Jesus makes a staving pronouncement concerning the consequences of imagination gone wild. He says:

> You have heard that it was said, 'You shall not commit adultery.' But I tell you that anyone who looks at a woman lustfully

has already committed adultery with her in his heart. If your right eye causes you to stumble, gouge it out and throw it away. It is better for you to lose one part of your body than for your whole body to be thrown into hell.

Matthew 5:27-29

Similarly, having hate in your heart for another is no small matter either. You may think that since you haven't actually did anything to the ones you hate, no harm has been done. However, nothing could be further from the truth. The Bible says, he that "hates his brother is [also] a murderer" (1 John 3:15). Holding on to hatred toward someone not only has negative physical consequences, but God sees harboring hate in your imagination as the spirit of murder.

Whether positive or negative, right or wrong, when it comes to the imagination, there are endless possibilities. However, one of its more glaring limitations is that it's vulnerable and very susceptible to external influences because it can't guard itself. It's exposed to all sensory information and input. In Proverbs 4:23 we are warned, "Above all else, guard your heart, for everything you do flows from it." In this passage, two words require defining. The first word is *heart,* and the second is *guard.* The word *heart* here isn't speaking of the cardio muscle (i.e. the physical heart), but is actually speaking of the mind. The word *guard* means to *protect, preserve and constantly monitor.* Guarding your heart is something you must do intentionally. You must filter everything that goes into your mind through the five senses, particularly that which comes through the eye and ear gates. Though you can't filter out everything, there are some things that you certainly should not be looking at or listening to.

For instance, when a person who plays video games visualizes himself committing acts of violence in a virtual environment it can, and often does, inspire them to commit these heinous acts in real life. Watching pornography is equally toxic because through the imagination, you're participating in the act in a virtual environment. That translates into extremely risky behaviors as the person tries to live out perverse fantasies in real life. This is why you can't allow the enemy to enter your imagination. If he enters your imagination, he has entered into your life. Proverbs 23:7 also informs us, "For as he thinketh in his heart, so is he" (KJV). Numerous case studies have revealed a common thread among mass murderers and sex offenders: they engaged in the activity at the imaginary level before they traveled down the road to committing these heinous acts.

THE IMAGINATION AND PERCEPTION

As we have discovered, the brain doesn't have the ability to separate thought from reality. Therefore, even if the sound is imagined, it alters your perception of the environment around you, and your mind interprets that something has really happened. A clear example of this phenomenon is found in 2 Kings, chapter 7. There we find four leprous men who were sitting on the outskirts of the city and having a conversation among themselves. Here's what they said: "Should we sit here and die or should we go into town and try to rustle up some food?" And the Lord says to them, "Go in, and I'm going to give you the food you need." These four leprous men are in the fourth stage of a debilitating disease that's tearing them apart.

They barely have any strength. Since their disease is highly contagious, incurable, and terminal, they've been banished from the community and were living in a leper colony. No one in society will have anything to do with them.

Being obedient to the Lord, these four leprous men start walking toward the enemy's camp. And as they started walking, the Lord caused the enemy to hear the sound of chariots and a great army. This so alarmed the enemy that they fled on foot, leaving behind their horses, food, clothing, weapons, gold, silver, and other valuables. This great army fled when no one was actually chasing them, all because they imagined they were hearing a greater army approaching.

Do you realize what that means for your own life? If you worship God when you're in your weakened state and not at your highest potential, God will intensify the sound of your worship so it will appear to the enemy that you're stronger than what you actually are. That's why when you give God glory, people around you think everything is alright. They think that you've made it through, and all is well. They have no idea you're in the weakest state you've ever been in. But every time you give God glory, it sounds like you're stronger than what you actually are.

However, none of this can happen unless you first do as the lepers did—respond to what you hear. If you're at home alone and you hear something in your sleep, you get up and listen for another sound. Then with caution, you look to see if you can find what caused the sound. When you've heard an authentic word from God, the next thing you ought to do is look to see what's moving, what's shifting, what's realigning. Though it may not have already come to pass, you should move forward as though you see it there in front of you.

IMAGINATION AND NEGATIVE PERCEPTION

Advertising executives and marketing psychologists have known for decades the power that optics and messaging play in persuading consumers to buy their products. Every year billions of dollars are spent on edgy and enticing television commercials and ad campaigns, all aimed at your brain and your pocketbook. And for good reason—it works. Whether it's for the latest model car or for a bowl of breakfast cereal, consumers are bombarded with strategic messaging, in every form of media that exists. Advertising executives know that what we see and what we hear can send our imaginations into overdrive in just a few seconds. Imagine the influence after long-term exposure. And the same optics and messaging used in marketing to build Fortune 500 companies also works in reverse—to kill, steal and destroy.

In 1 Samuel, chapter 17, we have a graphic example of the effects of negative perception. Verses 8-11 and 16 read as follows:

> Goliath stood and shouted to the ranks of Israel, "Why do you come out and line up for battle? Am I not a Philistine, and are you not the servants of Saul? Choose a man and have him come down to me. If he is able to fight and kill me, we will become your subjects; but if I overcome him and kill him, you will become our subjects and serve us." Then the Philistine said, "This day I defy the armies of Israel! Give me a man and let us fight each other." On hearing the Philistine's words, Saul and all the Israelites were dismayed and terrified. For forty days

the Philistine came forward every morning and evening and took his stand.

In this well-known biblical account of David and Goliath, Israel is facing defeat and servitude from a superior Philistine army. Goliath was the mammoth-sized Philistine warrior who stood nearly ten feet tall and could have weighed anywhere between 500 to 700 pounds.

Verse 16 tells us, "For forty days the Philistine came forward every morning and evening and took his stand." The Philistines had launched a very effective propaganda campaign that produced the desired effect: "Saul and all the Israelites were dismayed and terrified." Over thirty centuries later, military strategists still use propaganda and disinformation to try to confuse and discourage their enemy. The whole idea is to get the opponent to surrender or retreat with only a minimal amount of engagement.

As we learned from Dr. Ehrsson's experiments, what you see and hear will impact your perception, even if it's not true. The children of God were paralyzed and wouldn't fight because they believed the persuasive propaganda that no one could stand up to Goliath. When they thought about fighting, their minds reverted back to the threat and they would become immobilized, unable to defend what was theirs or pursue the promise. Their own minds were working against them. Like a roller-coaster that moves by perpetual motion (once it starts to move, it continues to move under its own force), Goliath's message of intimidation gave a push start. Israel's own fear took over and did the rest.

The enemy understands that if he manipulates your senses,

he manipulates your perception. Goliath got into the hearts and minds of the children of Israel and messed up their imagination, telling them morning, noon, and night for forty days what he was going to do and what they couldn't do. Remember that Goliath was almost ten feet tall. And as if his foreboding size weren't enough, he wore a bronze helmet and a bronze coat of scale armor that weighed approximately 125 pounds. His extensive arsenal included a javelin that was tipped with a fifteen-pound iron point (about the same weight as an Olympic shot-put). In fact, he had so many weapons that someone else had to carry his shield (verse 7). Yet, the Israelites were too rattled to think, "If Goliath is supposed to be such a champion, why does he need that many weapons?" The fact is that an insecure individual attempts to overcome their sense of low self-esteem and inadequacy by constantly overcompensating. When individuals don't really "have it" and know that they aren't really "all that," they readily boast in order to persuade people to like them, revere them, maybe even fear them. So, Goliath, who was supposed to be an undefeated champion, overcompensated with all these extra weapons.

For those of you who are boxing enthusiasts, you'll remember that Mike Tyson went into the ring wearing no socks. He was breaking all protocol because that wasn't considered the norm. In the ring, he wore no fancy robe, no socks, and as some have reported, no underwear! Unlike Goliath, it was Tyson's tenacious fighting technique, and not what he wore that did all the talking when the fight was on.

A real God-given champion doesn't have to have on a lot of

stuff. What makes you a heavyweight champion is that you're able to fight when you have nothing. Circumstances and people that surround you keep getting knocked out because they underestimate you. They're judging you based on what you have or don't have. Those who are hating on you, jealous of you, or lying on you don't understand what makes you a champion is that God is with you.

With all of Goliath's calculating plan to intimidate Israel into surrender, he left one small component out of his equation—a little shepherd boy named David, who knew that God was on his side. David shows up and Goliath has an immediate problem. David hasn't been there for those forty days, so he didn't get the memo that Goliath was going to annihilate the Israelites. While everyone else was already brainwashed, here was somebody that the enemy didn't intimidate.

So David messes up the enemy's strategy because his imagination hasn't been molested by Goliath's propaganda. The other Israelites have succumbed psychologically to the enemy's threat. However, when David shows up with lunch and overhears the enemy spouting out threats, it has the opposite effect on him. Instead of being afraid, David said, "Put me in the fight." Everybody else said, "Man, you can't fight him. You see how big he is?" David's response is, "No matter how big my enemy is; I've got a God that's bigger than that. So that makes Goliath, just a little ol' giant." This is how we must deal with all of our harassing giants! You should always say, "Greater is he that is in me, than he that is in the world. God is bigger than my bills. He's bigger than my haters. He's bigger than my mistakes. Since God is bigger, then they're all just little ol' giants!"

I don't know whether you realize it or not, but anatomically bumblebees aren't supposed to be able to fly. Their wings are too short, and their bodies are too heavy. Scientists are still baffled as to how bumblebees with those little wings can carry all that weight through the air. But they fly because God told them they could fly, and they navigate without a GPS or compass, all because of what God said. No one has ever limited their possibilities with disinformation and doubt about what they could and couldn't do. If God said it, that settles it. God's Word is the only thing that can make the impossible and the improbable become possible.

David Gets Involved

It's amazing how God, through our own life experiences, is preparing us for our divine purpose. Oftentimes, God introduces us to a particular circumstance so that He can set us up for our destiny. God may not call you through a star in the night sky, a burning bush, or an upper room experience. Nevertheless, God can send you to complete a seemingly mundane task that will trigger His master plan for your life. God's ways are not our ways, but regardless of how He does it, He is taking you to that exceeding abundant place in life. That thing that God has you doing right now may place you on the doorstep of your destiny.

So, how did God get David involved? Continuing with the text, verses 17-19 inform us:

Now Jesse said to his son David, "Take this ephah of roasted grain and these ten loaves of bread for your brothers and hurry to their camp. Take along these ten cheeses to the commander of their unit. See how your brothers are and bring back some assurance from them. They are with Saul and all the men of Israel in the Valley of Elah, fighting against the Philistines.

Jesse sent David to do two seemingly mundane things: drop off some lunch and bring back some assurance as to how things were going in this military campaign against the Philistines. Jesse set the context for David's little errand when he said, "They are with Saul ... fighting against the Philistines." However, when David arrived at the front-line where all the action is supposed to be, he's thrown off. He was under the impression that he was going to the battleground. In his mind, he imagined that he would be hearing the clanking of swords, the butting of shields and the sounds of the enemy being slaughtered. But, when he gets to the battleground, he doesn't hear anything. David must have asked himself, what's wrong with this picture?

As Christians, we're in the army of the Lord. However, the communities in which our churches and congregations are in are confused about us calling ourselves the army of Christ. You claim that you're in God's army, but when they come by the church, they hear no sound of warfare. In God's camp, there ought to be some sounds from warriors who have come through a hellified week of having to fight for their sanity and peace of mind. The world ought to be hearing people who are crying to God, saying "I'm in the fight of my life. I don't care who doesn't like me shouting. I'm praising God any how!"

When David arrives at the front line, he's baffled. If the enemy is being defeated, why doesn't it sound like warfare? David must have been thinking, "We're the people of the Most High God. Why aren't we putting our feet on the enemy's neck?" David then asks, "Who's the uncircumcised Philistine that defies the armies of the Lord?" Here's where we see David having the audacity to face a better-equipped army, not based on military might, but on the fact that Israel was in relationship with God. The Lord would not have His people who are called by His name serving the Philistines, instead of El Elyon, the Most High God.

David began to see how what he had been doing all the time was really preparation to step into his destiny. While the rest of Israel was going through boot camp, practicing military exercises, and learning the art of war, David was in the wilderness and meadows learning to fight a different type of giant. He was learning hand-to-hand combat by killing ferocious wild animals, like a bear and a lion, in order to protect his flock. It's important to understand that David wasn't just indiscriminately killing these animals. Had the lion and the bear minded their own business and kept on going, they would have made it home to their cubs. However, when they crossed the line and tried to attack the sheep David was tending to, the other side of the shepherd boy came out. Humble little David was fearless when it came to protecting his sheep. That was the training that David needed to prepare him for the battle with Goliath.

Many of you are going through some challenging circumstances right now, and you have no idea why God has you walking that road. But I'm writing this book just to let you know that there is a purpose in your pain. Keep walking by faith, because God is taking you somewhere. He's bringing you to an expected destination where there is fullness of joy. You're not merely meandering through life, but you're on a path that leads to your destiny.

There are some other elements in this text that will help us understand why Goliath's threats didn't have a negative influence on David. In verses 23-27 the text reads:

> As he was talking with them, Goliath, the Philistine champion from Gath, stepped out from his lines and shouted his usual defiance, and David heard it. Whenever the Israelites saw the man, they all fled from him in great fear. Now the Israelites had been saying, "Do you see how this man keeps coming out? He comes out to defy Israel. The king will give great wealth to the man who kills him. He will also give him his daughter in marriage and will exempt his family from taxes in Israel." David asked the men standing near him, "What will be done for the man who kills this Philistine and removes this disgrace from Israel? Who is this uncircumcised Philistine that he should defy the armies of the living God?" They repeated to him what they had been saying and told him, "This is what will be done for the man who kills him."

The first observation is that David never heard Goliath's forty days of threats. It's important that we stop listening to all of the negative information that the enemy throws at us to paralyze us. If he can get you to the point where you won't lift a finger to defend yourself, he knows that the battle is already won. In the face of overwhelming odds, greatness occurs when people have not internalized someone else's criticism, negativity, and pessimism. When it comes to others telling you what you can't do, what is impossible, or what has never been done before, don't listen. Your confession should always be, "I can do all things through Christ that strengthens me."

Secondly, David understood that the Philistines were uncircumcised. To the Jews, there was no other rite as important as circumcision. Abraham, the father of the Jews, was the first to be circumcised and his son Isaac was the first child to be circumcised. Circumcision was a sign of God's everlasting covenant that He made with Abraham and all his posterity. In this Abrahamic covenant, there are perpetual blessings and promises based upon the faithfulness of God to His people. David correctly evaluated the circumstances when he asked, "Who is this uncircumcised Philistine that he should defy the armies of the living God?" David knew that his people were in covenant relationship with the "living God," and God would not tolerate a Philistine encroachment of Israel's covenantal rights, blessings, and promises. Therefore, David stood firm in his faith because he knew *who* he was and *whose* he was.

Thirdly, David engaged his imagination when he heard the reward for defeating Goliath. When David overheard this bit of information, he basically asked, "Could you just say that one more time please?" The chance to receive great wealth, marry the king's fine daughter (which also means becoming the king's son-in-law, an immediate promotion over his older brothers), and get tax-exempt status for him and his family for life made David's imagination and determination kick into overdrive. He said, "Oh yeah, I can see myself being blessed like that after taking care of this Philistine."

David imagined himself being rich enough to buy his father a new house and being a blessing to others. He could see himself being a member of the royal family, having a suite at the palace, and eating at the king's table. David imagined having a fine wife and living in a mansion with gardens, groves, and pools. David could see himself having plenty money and never having to pay taxes again. He saw beyond the giant and into the place of God's blessings. Whenever you have God's promises, preparation, opportunity, imagination, and determination all working together, that's a satisfaction-guaranteed formula for success.

We can't see God. We can't see faith, and we can't see the future. But if you have the radical faith to worship God in the face of all your ugly giants, the God of all possibility is getting ready to give you the victory. Whatever was shut down to you, God is getting ready to give it back to you. Whatever you were rejected from, whatever you didn't qualify for, God is canceling everything negative you've heard in the last forty days. Because of the sacrifice at Calvary, the blood of Jesus has canceled everything negative you have been through in the last forty days. Give God the glory, and dance like David danced!

Three
IMAGINATION VERSUS FACTS

In the Charles Dickens fictional classic *Hard Times*, the reader is introduced to a sinister schoolmaster named Thomas Gradgrind. In this story, Gradgrind plants a skewed philosophy on education that has cross-pollinated from Dickens's literary landscape into much of America's public school system. Gradgrind insisted that the teachers under his employ, "Teach these boys and girls nothing but facts. Facts alone are all they are going to need in life. Plant nothing in them but facts and root out everything else. You can only form the minds of an unreasoning animal with facts. Anything outside of facts will never be beneficial to them."

Disturbingly, this distorted methodology is not only found in classrooms throughout the country, but it has also meandered its way into churches and sanctuaries alike. Focusing in on facts leaves very little room for faith. Facts suggest that this is how it is, and this is how it will remain. When you're given just facts, it reinforces what is and leaves very little room for imagination to surmise what could be. This is why people who are devoid of imagination readily hold fast to facts.

A fact is something that has occurred or is actually the case. A fact is always predicated and based on something that has already happened. A fact is not futuristic and is always based on the past. Thus, facts are limited because they have no answer or information for the future. The litmus test of a fact is that it has verifiability, which means that it can be proven to correspond with an experience. You can't tell what a fact is if you don't have an experience with it. In scientific circles, facts are verified by repeatable experiments and predictable results.

In elementary schools, countless children have been exposed to a fact-based instruction. This is an imagination-suppressing method. A select group of high-ranking educators, social scientists, and academicians who develop educational literature for our schools decided for us all that knowing facts should be the primary goal of classroom instruction. And because the facts we're taught and are often outgrowths of someone else's agenda, we wind up only knowing what they say we should know. So we're fed facts such as: the Mississippi River is the longest river in the United States; Mount Everest is the highest mountain in the world and the Great Wall of China is the longest structure ever built by humans. Someone who you'll never know has determined that these are the kinds of things your children should know.

When curriculums reinforce memorization, it sacrifices imagination. Educational regimentation circumvents freedom and individuality as well. The teacher taught you what the highest mountain in the world is and what country it's in. However, she never told you how beautiful Mount Everest's snow-capped peak is amongst the backdrop of the crystal blue sky. On Friday when test day came, the more facts you answered correctly, the better grade you received. If you received a 100 percent, you were considered to be smart. If you received below 65 percent, you were told that you failed, regardless of the fact that you were brilliant, creative, and full of ingenuity. However, the test didn't measure those attributes. This is the dilemma with fact-based instruction—it leaves no room for ingenuity and imagination.

Nowadays, a student may not be concerned with the mere memorization of the "so-called" facts in class because there's no challenge set before them. The student becomes restless and agitated because the subject matter fails to engage him, and he is unable to connect with the curriculum. How to manage their boredom becomes the greatest challenge to the student. When the same child begins acting out on their frustration they invariably get labeled as a trouble maker, when the real problem is the under-qualified teacher failed to recognize the attributes of a gifted student. This gifted child is then evaluated by an overworked school social worker and before it is all over, ends up with an ADHD (Attention Deficit Hyperactivity Disorder) diagnosis and a prescription for Ritalin.

On the other hand, in many underserved communities through the United States, you'll find underperforming schools, putting out underperforming students who are then funneled into low-earning jobs that relegate them to becoming disenfranchised consumers who never get ahead. This is not by accident, but by design. It's an indictment of our public school system. Think about it, if a high school is designated as a "College Prep" to matriculate students through college, then what's the goal of a high school that's not college prep? If college prep schools feed into institutions of higher learning, then into what institutions or career paths do general high schools feed students? Unfortunately, for many students, these under-functioning schools are conduits to correctional and penal institutions. With zero-tolerance school discipline policies, black males are much more likely to be suspended and expelled than white students. Once they're out of the school, the likelihood of them dropping out and becoming involved with the penal system increases exponentially. For those that do graduate from an underperforming school, they have only learned enough *facts* to graduate, but not enough *truth* to succeed in life.

Truth is greater than facts. For example, in the Gospel of St. John, Jesus was on trial before Pontius Pilate. Pilate said, "Do you refuse to speak to me?" He stated the facts to Jesus, saying, "Don't you realize I have power either to free you or to crucify you?" However, Pilate's facts were not the whole story because Jesus retorted with the truth: "You would have no power over me if it were not given to you from above." There's always more to the story than just the facts. Truth is greater than facts, because facts focus on particulars, whereas truth considers everything. The truth will make you free. Facts are used to manage your mind. Facts incarcerate ideas. They put a cap on possibilities. Facts are for bean counters and bankers—but not for believers. Believers may start with facts, but as soon as you factor in the truth, you'll learn to trust in God, with whom all things are possible.

TIME TO BE TESTED

Drawing once again from a classroom analogy, in order to bring you to the place of maturity and perfection, it becomes necessary for God to have you go through certain tests. And just as in the classroom, whenever we're not getting it, He keeps retesting us until we pass. He tests us until we learn that whatever He said is true. Therefore, God tests us so we'll stop testing Him and learn to trust Him at His Word. We have to learn how to believe without doubting, because no matter what we go through, His grace is always sufficient. Throughout your walk with God, you will find that trials are God's way to prove that whatever He has promised you are *His* facts. If there is anyone who has the facts, it's God. He knows all things and His facts are not stuck in the past, because He writes history in advance. Therefore, you don't have to be so concerned about the devil, because the devil is already defeated. Whenever the devil reminds you about your past, you remind him what Revelation 20 says about his future. God is beyond the boundaries of time, and He already is in the future, where the devil has been condemned eternally.

Unfortunately, the future is not observable in the natural. What we know as facts is limited to what is observable and testable. In order to test observable phenomena or prove a hypothesis, scientists have developed what's called the "scientific method." The scientific method consists of four stages: characterization, hypothesis, prediction, and experimentation.

The first stage of the scientific method you learned in middle school is *characterization*. Characterization is empirical and comes from observation that involves looking at and assessing some observable phenomena. However, in the spiritual realm, every now and then, God makes you go through something where you can't respond or react. You just have to step back and observe to see what in the world is going on. "How did I end up like this?" "What in the world happened in my life to bring me to this point," are questions that have cross your mind. Many of you are in a season of observation. This is where uncertainty exists, and you can't get a handle on what to do, so you just observe.

The second step in the scientific method is *hypothesis*. The *American Heritage Dictionary* defines hypothesis as "a tentative explanation that accounts for a set of facts that can be tested by further investigation; a theory." A hypothesis can also be framed as "a hypothetical explanation as to what is happening." However, in the book of Job, we see some hypotheses being bandied about by Job's friends. After Job had lost everything, his three friends came around, criticizing him. "Maybe it's your fault. You had to do something to enrage God. Obviously, you're in this position because of some terrible sin you've committed," they inaccurately theorized. Just as Job's friends did, we also theorize when we say things like, "Why in the world did God take momma? If I'm this nice, why in the world do I not have that many friends? If I'm such a loving person, why am I still by myself? Why is it that even though I'm looking so hard, I can't find a job? Why has sickness invaded my body, when I'm trying to live and do right?" When we're not sure of the reasons why something has occurred, we begin to theorize.

Interestingly, as it pertains to Job's situation, the text tells us that there was also some hypothesis in heaven as well. In the first chapter of Job, we find the following account in verses 7-12.

> The LORD said to Satan, "Where have you come from?" Satan answered the LORD, "From roaming throughout the earth, going back and forth on it." Then the LORD said to Satan, "Have you considered my servant Job? There is no one on earth like him; he is blameless and upright, a man who fears God and shuns evil." "Does Job fear God for nothing?" Satan replied. "Have you not put a hedge around him and his household and everything he has? You have blessed the work of his hands, so that his flocks and herds are spread throughout the land. But now stretch out your hand and strike everything he has, and he will surely curse you to your face." The LORD said to Satan, "Very well, then, everything he has is in your power, but on the man himself do not lay a finger."

Here we can see that Satan had a theory concerning Job's faithfulness toward God. Satan's theory was that since God had a protective hedge around all that Job had, and since God had exceedingly abundantly blessed Job, those were the only reasons Job served God. Satan's hypothesis was, "Does Job fear God for nothing?" In other words, the devil was saying that Job only serves God, because God has spoiled him by giving him a whole bunch of stuff.

However, the devil also has a theory for each one of us who have been called according to God's purpose. His theory is that if he could just illegitimize your imagination, he can negate the fulfillment of your dreams. However, from the minute the devil placed you in his sights to destroy you, his theory has proven to have an innate error. He came up short because he left out the "faith factor." Though the devil may have you in his crosshairs, if you can just look beyond your dilemma and focus on your dreams, he can't stop you from reaching your destiny.

The third step in the scientific method is *prediction*. In prediction, you state what you believe is going to happen. For example, the weatherman can only predict the weather. He really doesn't know for sure what the weather is going to be. Predictions by nature are uncertain. Again, going back to Job's temptation, the devil's prediction was, "But now stretch out your hand and strike everything he has, and he will surely curse you to your face." Yes, you may be in the midst of one of the most difficult trials of your life. And the devil is predicting that you'll give up and turn your back on God. The devil said that Job would curse God to his face. However, this is only a prediction. The devil doesn't hold tomorrow in his hands. He can't control the outcomes, and he doesn't really know what you are going to do.

However, God doesn't predict. He prophesies. Whatever God says shall surely come to pass, fret not—God is going to work it out for you. The Bible says, "...all things work together for good to those who love God, to those are called according to His purpose" (Romans 8:28 NKJV). It's not that all things are going to work out somehow. That would only be a prediction. The Word says that all things will work together for the "good." That means a good God has predetermined and decreed a good outcome for all the things that the world, the flesh, and the devil can throw at you. God doesn't predict. God prophesies.

The fourth step is *experimentation* and *testing*. Everyone goes through a season of testing. It's never a matter of *if* you'll be tested, but it's a matter of *when* you'll be tested. When an automobile manufacturer produces a new model of cars, they build the vehicles to meet certain performance and safety standards. However, in order to prove the automobiles can meet the manufacturer's specifications, every aspect of the cars must be tested and retested before they pass quality assurance and are sold to the public.

Similarly, when it comes to the life of a believer, we too, go through a series of tests and retests. However, the test is not only for the person going through it. God's tests have multifunction purposes. As we have examined in Job's case, his test was a result of God's challenge to Satan. God asked him, "Have you considered my servant Job? There is no one on earth like him; he is blameless and upright, a man who fears God and shuns evil." Here we clearly see a heavenly purpose behind Job's testing from God, Satan, and from people on earth.

In Job's testing, God proved something to Satan that the devil has never really understood—the dynamics of a love relationship. The Bible tells us that God is love. Love is an intrinsic, necessary aspect of God's person. It's not an attribute with

God. Love is His essence. Satan can't comprehend or operate within the context of love because it's not a part of his make-up. With Satan, externals are important: the lust of the eye, the lust of the flesh, and the pride of life. These were the three areas where he tempted Eve in the Garden and Jesus in the wilderness. Therefore, God allowed Satan to throw Job into this test to prove to him that a love relationship is deeper than a relationship based on externals like wealth and even health. Job may have cursed the day that he was born, but he never cursed God. Job said, "Though he slay me, yet will I hope in him; I will surely defend my ways to his face. Indeed, this will turn out for my deliverance" (Job 13:15-16a). With that, Job passed the test!

Job's testing was to prove to his three hypocritical friends, that he was going to come through his situation victoriously. It's the same with you and me. Just as He had to show Job's friends, God is taking you through a test just to show your naysayers that you were worth the investment. He's taking you through the test just to show the world what He can do with an underdog. Though He may throw you in the midst of the fiery furnace, it's not to destroy you but to temper you and make you better. Therefore, you can feel good about what God is doing in your life. Your triumphant testimony is "I passed the test!"

Your critics will still be wagging their tongues. They're pointing at the mistakes you made. They try to distract you from a victory by causing you to focus on a moot point. But you can tell your haters that just because you've passed the test, that doesn't mean you didn't get some stuff wrong. It doesn't mean I did everything right. You don't have to ace the test in order to pass. They're wondering how you passed the test. So tell them, in this test, I was able to open up the textbook to get the right answers. In the middle of the test, God will let you refer to the textbook (the Bible). Open up the textbook to Romans 8:37-39, where Paul covers the whole gamut of suffering. To all of it he says:

> No, in all these things we are more than conquerors through him who loved us. For I am convinced that neither death nor life, neither angels nor demons, neither the present nor the future, nor any powers, neither height nor depth, nor anything else in all creation, will be able to separate us from the love of God that is in Christ Jesus our Lord.

Finally, the most important reason why God sent Job through this test was for you, me, and everyone else who has learned about the trials of Job. God sent Job through his test to help us understand how God works in midst of our trials. God allowed Job to go through living hell, just to bring him back better than he was before, so we could have an example of how to trust God in all of our difficulties.

In the final analysis, we've learned that facts don't have the last say so. God does. When the facts of life present themselves, whether they're trials, tribulations, or giants, know that, "No weapon that is formed against thee shall prosper; and every tongue that shall rise against thee in judgment thou shalt condemn."

Four
PICTURE ME

It was French philosopher Michel de Montaigne, who in his book, *The Complete Essays*, wrote "the most terrible and violent of our afflictions is to despise our own beings." In his examination of why people are susceptible to self-hatred, Montaigne postulated that we're all surrounded by the wrong role models, which don't give space to what most of us are really like. Consequently, self-hatred or low self-esteem occurs because we can't measure up to the role-model's image. An example of Montaigne's observations is played out all over the world with women who are in bondage to eating disorders like anorexia and bulimia. Unfortunately, many women have gotten a picture in their mind of being rail-thin like some model they've seen on the cover of an upscale fashion magazine. The tragic thing about that picture is that the model doesn't actually look like that because the photo has been manipulated by computer programs like Photoshop. Nevertheless, it gets internalized and becomes the model image in that woman's mind. Now she tortures her body by starvation and purging, trying to become a replica of an unrealistic image, all because she hates who she really is.

It's amazing how our ancestors never considered self-esteem. Being so absorbed with survival, they never had a moment to wonder, "Do I like myself?" Self-esteem is a somewhat modern Western culture phenomenon. For most of human history, the very idea of it was unexplored. In most societies and cultures, the individual was secondary to the advancement of the whole. Your highs and lows were contingent on the success or victory of your village, tribe or nation. The collective identity was the most important thing.

For thousands of years, books have been written and published. Most of these books are centered on various topics such as fiction, poetry, history, politics, warfare, conquerors, and monarchs. But it wasn't until the late seventies or early eighties that books about self-esteem were in large measure introduced into the culture. Many believed that awareness of self-esteem would cure societal ills like crime, addiction, and poor education. In the wake of this effort, a multi-billion dollar industry ensued; yet, the results still have not paid off. In fact, to the contrary, many recent studies have concluded that high self-esteem has contributed to aggression. High self-esteem is a key factor for narcissism. High self-esteem is a secret ingredient for elitism. High self-esteem can, in fact, be found in classism. Many people love themselves to death, to the point that they give no care or concern about other people. They so love who they are that they have forgotten that they have a commandment to love humanity.

In the book entitled *Unworthy: How to Stop Hating Yourself*, the author picturesquely describes that there is little connection between self-esteem and reality. Sometimes the people we assume would hate themselves do not. You would be amazed at how many burglars, murderers, rapists, and muggers feel good about themselves. Career criminals such as these are sociopaths who actually believe that there's nothing wrong with killing a person for their money because they were hungry. In their sick minds, the value of another person's life doesn't factor into their equation. Only that person's money and their sociopathic needs do. On the other hand, many with stellar characteristics can't stand themselves. After having released eleven CDs, having acted in five major motion pictures, and having garnered over two hundred music awards, in an exclusive interview, Mariah Carey confessed, "I've always had low self-esteem. And the reality is, while most people don't know it and can't tell, I still do."

After the Golden Globe Awards, the plus-size actress Gabourey Sidibe of *Precious* fame was targeted on Twitter and Facebook by people ranting about how she looked. In retaliation, the star tweeted back, "To people making mean comments about my size, my shape, my color and my hair at the Golden Globe Awards, I most definitely cried about it…on my private jet, flying on my way back to my million-dollar dream job." That's self-esteem. Many of us would assume that Mariah Carey would be the one with high self-esteem, and Gabourey Sidibe would be the one who was absent of it.

Social media have inundated us with opportunities to flaunt our own "self-esteem" through the recent phenomenon called "selfies." Added to the dictionary in 2013, the term "selfie" refers to a type of self-portrait typically taken on a camera phone and posted on social media. Psychologists suggest that many people pose for and post selfies as an attempt to feel better about themselves. After uploading their picture, they take every "like" on Facebook, Instagram, and Twitter as an affirmation and will get upset if you don't "like" their picture. The portraits are to project an idyllic existence that really doesn't exist. How else could you be the photographer and the model and purport the picture to be a legitimate portrait? How in the world can you possibly be objective about yourself when you're the lighting director, the editor, and you have the final say on what pictures to post? You can't.

Many people who take pictures of themselves all day long really don't like looking at themselves, but they want other people to look at them. And the more people press the "like" button, the more they're affirmed in their own broken low self-esteem, thinking, "If a number of people say it looks nice, then I must look nice." However, it doesn't matter how many people like your picture if when you look at yourself, you don't like what you see.

Not only do many who are in show business or who are social media fanatics suffer from low self-esteem, but we also find that there are people in the Church who have *spiritual* low self-esteem. However, it's vitally important to know that God wants you to see a picture of yourself, using the lens of divine intention. That means you can't get the correct picture of yourself from a selfie. Neither can you get the right picture of yourself from a movie star or a magazine cover. According to Genesis, we were made in God's image and His likeness. Though there is much to say about man being made in the image of God, let it suffice for this study to say that "in His image" means, that we were made with communicable attributes of God. Man could function in the context of personhood, having a will, emotions, intellect, morality, creativity, the ability to love and receive love, to operate in authority, to exercise dominion, to judge, conceptualize, reason, and prosper. In other words, God has an image of you that fits within the context of His design and purpose for your life—it's His picture of you.

A lot of people are going to be unnerved, disturbed, and upset because they want to keep putting you in the picture of your past. But God is getting ready to take a moving picture of what your glorious future is getting ready to look like. The reason why the enemy has been fighting you so ferociously is because he has already seen a picture of your destiny, and he wants to kill you before you can become what you've been dreaming about. But no devil in hell can wipe away the picture God has placed in your mind.

YOUR DIVINE PHOTO SHOOT

Instagram is one of today's most popular social networking websites where you can post photos on the Internet. On

Instagram, the pictures you post can be adjusted with sixteen different filters which change the texture of the picture. Interestingly, some of these Instagram filters can be paralleled with our own circumstances as it pertains to the image that we have of ourselves or that others portray to us. The first of these photo-finishing filters is called *Rise.* God says regardless of what picture you have in your mind concerning where you are right now; get ready to rise to a higher level. God wants us to rise to that exceeding abundant place of blessing. The Lord wants us to prosper and be in health, even as our soul prospers. Though you may have formed a picture in your mind about your current circumstances, get ready to rise when you see the picture God is about to take of you.

The second filter is called *Sierra.* It gives a faded look to the picture. When I think of the word "Sierra," I think of a section of the Mojave Desert called the Sierra Desert. Many of your haters are relishing over the fact that you're in a dry and desolate place in your life. In their picture of you, they expect you just to fade away into insignificance. However, if they're hating on you while you're in a desert season, what will they do when you come out of your "sierra" situation and into the oasis that God is going to bless you with? None of your haters and critics understands that your desert season is only temporary. Though they may have a picture of you during your desert season, wait until they compare your before and after photos. They thought their picture of you was the only true picture of you. But God has another picture of you that uses the filter of His promises to bless you exceeding abundantly, above all, that you can ask or even think. Your before and after photo will not even be able to be compared. God has a divine image of you that trials, tribulations, and your haters simply cannot filter out.

Another Instagram filter is called *1977*. It's a throwback. A lot of people who don't like you always want to put you through the filter of your past. However, I want to confirm a word of encouragement that the apostle Paul said to the Corinthian church. "Therefore if any man be in Christ, he is a new creature: old things are passed away; behold, all things are become new" (2 Corinthians 5:17 KJV). I know some of you have difficulty shutting out the images of the past, where pictures of who you use to be flash across the canvas of your mind. However, there's something you can do to destroy all those negatives—those dark, dingy images—of your past. You have to forget what lies behind, and press forward towards the mark of the prize of the high calling in God. It doesn't matter what happened yesterday; it won't stop my tomorrow.

The final filter is the one that most people don't use. It's called *Normal*. The reason people don't typically use this filter is because they're not satisfied with how their picture looks naturally. They prefer the enhancements that the other filters offer. In life, just as it is with the Instagram filters, people are not satisfied with who they are naturally and try to impress others with an enhanced picture. However, the only way to find satisfaction and fulfillment is by being content with who you are naturally. As we learned from Montaigne's theory, people try to imitate the wrong role models. They try to project themselves using imagery that's not naturally theirs. In the final analysis, this never works because you can only be good at being you. Your happiness must be from within and not contingent upon someone else's acceptance. When you're content with being and doing you, only then can you excel to be whom God called you to be.

Normal is good because it means that your life isn't being distorted by the "chaos" filters encountered in life. The normal filter represents blocking out the chaotic circumstances that have been dogging your steps. After having gone through some of the toughest situations in your life, it's a blessing to finally return to normal. You just want to go to work and mind your business. You just want to be able to sleep through the night without receiving any disturbing phone calls. Where your prayer used to be "Lord, make my life normal," now your testimony is, "Lord, thank you for letting me be myself again!"

The normal filter also coincides with the concept of *restoration*. As David said of God in Psalm 23:3; "He restoreth my soul" (KJV). The word *restoreth* means to "return to the starting point, to take it back to how it used to be." Not long ago, there was a homeless man who won a million-dollar state lottery. In an instant, this homeless, indigent man became the talk of the town and everyone's friend. Soon he was overwhelmed with all of the long-lost relatives and friends who, a few days earlier, wouldn't have given him the time of day. But now that he was temporarily rich, leaches came out of the woodwork. After being drained of most of his money, this man hooked up with the wrong people and was murdered for what little money he had left. However, before he died, he was interviewed on a local television news station. The reporter asked, "How is life since you won all that money?" To everyone's surprise, his response was, "I just want my life back." This poor soul went through so much chaos after having won that money, that all he wanted was to be back to normal—a homeless man that no one cared to know.

No Filters, Just Favor

Before we delve into the three aspects of God's photo shoot of favor, let's define the word *favor*. Of the many definitions, the one that I like the most is: "unfair partiality." As my friend and ministerial colleague Bishop T.D. Jakes would say, "Favor ain't fair." To be fair means to treat everyone the same way; to be impartial. However, that isn't the case for favor. Favor demands *unfair* partiality. This means the recipient receives favor that is completely undeserved, and that gives him an unfair advantage over others. When God's favor is upon you, miracles, promotion, and blessings happen, regardless of your qualifications, education, knowledge, place in line, or ability. When God bestows His favor upon you, it's with willful intentionality. He loves you and simply wants to bless you so that He gets all the glory. God will make it a point to skip over others just to bless you. That's favor!

There are three important aspects that are necessary to know about God's photo shoot of favor. The first one is "no filter." The favor on your life doesn't require a filter. You won't have to go through anything in order to possess the manifestation of what God promised. Folks are going to be baffled because they can't understand how you have achieved this level of success without having to compromise who you are in God. The reason why the enemy can't stand you is because you don't have to put on airs; you don't have to be phony; you don't have to pretend like you're somebody you're not.

The second thing you have to be mindful of in regards to your favor photo shoot is "no frame." With the emergence of camera phones, sales for picture frames have gone down tremendously because most people who take pictures with their smart phones never print them. You're satisfied just scanning through them on your phone or leaving them on your computer. Similarly, the reason your adversarial forces are going to be frustrated is that they don't know how to frame you. They keep trying to put you in a box, but every time they try to limit your potential, your gift, and your intelligence, God keeps breaking their frame. Some of you can start thanking God now that you're getting ready to walk into an area of life you didn't know you had the gift to operate. That's because a supernatural God is opening doors for you that your haters can't shut.

By nature, frames impose limits and set predetermined boundaries. Frames are also stationary and designed to be hung or set in one place. This is why when God orchestrates your favor photo shoot, there is no frame. Frames fix you to a particular place. However, the anointing on your life is so fluid that folks won't be able to nail you down. When they think they have you cornered in one area, God is shifting you into another place. Your adversarial forces can't box you in because the gift on your life is so heavy. God is getting ready to give you wisdom, knowledge, and foresight for which you received no training. All you will know is that the favor on your life is so fresh that every time they try to box you in, God writes a new job description for the anointing that is on your life.

The third and final thing is, "no flaws." Your adversarial forces have always been looking to find a fault with you that they can exploit. However, since you have the favor of God, you are as wise as serpents but harmless as a dove. The only thing they can say is, "I find no fault in him." Therefore, they hate you without a cause. But it doesn't faze you, because of God's favor. When you get to that level of freedom, it doesn't matter what they think of you. It doesn't matter what they say behind your back because you like being you, even if they can't stand you. In Nikki Giovanni's poem *Ego Tripping*, she says, "I sowed diamonds in my back yard." She also asserts, "I am so hip that even my errors are correct." We are children of the Most High God. We're kingdom kids, and our Father works out all things for our good. Tell your haters, "Don't get it mixed up. I don't have a self-esteem issue. I don't have an attitude problem. But what I do have is unshakable faith and assurance that if God be for me, who can stand against me? My heavenly Father said that no weapon formed against me shall prosper."

PICTURE YOURSELF PROSPEROUS

In Judges, chapter 6, God is chastising the children of Israel because they backslid when they started reverencing the gods of the Amorites. Since they didn't honor God in their worship, God put them in the hands of the Midianites, whom He gave providential license to oppress Israel. However, a very critical point is found in Judges 6:6 where it says: "Midian so impoverished the Israelites that they cried out to the Lord for help."

The children of God didn't cry out to Him when they were under attack. They only started to cry out to Him when they became impoverished. It's not God's will to turn a deaf ear to His children not having enough to eat, not being able to do what they want to do for their family, having to make secondary choices that don't match their potential, or having to settle for second rate when they're operating with a first-class anointing. This is why David said, "I have been young, and now am old; yet have I not seen the righteous forsaken, nor his seed begging bread" (Psalm 37:25 KJV). In Israel, God made provisions for the poor, so that they wouldn't have to have beggars (see Leviticus 19:9-10; Deuteronomy 24:19-21). Nevertheless, to be poverty stricken was a curse (see Deuteronomy 28:15-68).

Yes, the enemy may oppress you. Yes, he may also harass you. Yes, he may even attack you. However, the enemy crosses the line when he makes you impoverished. As a child of God, you are not supposed to be financially struggling. When the enemy starts messing with your money, do as Israel did—cry out to God. It's not the intention, the mind or the heart of God for His child to picture themselves poor. God says, "This is not in accordance to the will that I have for your life." Some of you are not going to get this breakthrough because you think it's wrong to ask God about money. You think that way because you are limited by your own perception of what other people think. When you do that, you're blocking the hand of God from reaching you.

However, God says, "If you're tired of being under financial duress; tired of being behind on your bills; tired of always having to rob Peter to pay Paul; the only reason I haven't moved is because you forgot to ask Me to give you the finances you need." In James 4:2, the Bible says, "...You covet but you cannot get what you want, so you quarrel and fight. You do not have because you do not ask God." Asking God is an exercise of faith, and without faith, it is impossible to please God.

Picture yourself being debt free. Picture yourself being a millionaire. Picture yourself living life more abundantly. Picture your cup running over. Picture yourself being the lender and not the borrower. The Bible says, "It is more blessed to give than to receive" (Acts 20:35). This is true, not only because giving makes you feel all warm and fuzzy on the inside. The fact is giving and receiving are on two opposite ends. The giving end is better because you can't give what you don't have. Therefore, you must be blessed already in order to be a giver. Giving is also better because you're functioning in an image of God's attribute. God is a giver, and because of that, He loves a cheerful giver (2 Corinthians 9:7). Picture yourself giving someone a home. Picture yourself buying someone a car. Picture yourself paying someone's tuition. Picture yourself paying off someone's bills. Picture yourself as being prosperous enough to help someone else and your church prosper.

In Judges 6:7, when the people cried out to God, He began to move. The Scriptures tell us that He sent an angel to a man named Gideon. When the angel appeared, Gideon was threshing wheat in a winepress. This was odd because what Gideon was assigned to do, did not match the place where he was doing it. You thresh wheat in a barn. You make wine in a winepress.

Just like Gideon, many people are frustrated because where you work doesn't match the call of God on your life. However, I'm writing this book to encourage you that if you're occupationally out of alignment, it's the assignment of God to put you in a place where you can work your gift. Those of you who are believing God for a transfer, get ready for favor to transport you to your place of prosperity. But you must be willing to examine yourself and your circumstances realistically.

Why was Gideon threshing wheat in a winepress? It's because whenever there was a harvest, the enemy (the Midianites) came and took it. Many of us today are hiding our gift from the enemy, but doing that places us out of purpose. Whenever we're functioning out of purpose, fulfillment isn't possible, and advancement is stifled. A racehorse doesn't make the best workhorse. They can adapt, but they won't be fulfilled or at their best in an occupation where they are not pursuing their purpose.

Like Gideon, whenever we're not functioning in our gift, God can't get the glory out of our lives. Whether we're out of place and forced to function in the mundane, or we're bogged down because of the attacks of the enemy, we must not allow circumstances or the enemy to suppress who God called us to be. If the enemy can get you to buy into his picture of you and have you conform to the wrong image, you'll never actualize your dreams. Many of us are frustrated because we, like Gideon, are stuck in the wrong frame. Instead of fighting the enemy, we often end up hiding from the enemy and not using our gift. Walking in God's purpose and plan is where all the power for living a victorious life and fulfilling your destiny lies.

God had to help Gideon recognize who he really was. God had to remove all those negative filters and destroy the enemy's frame to show Gideon the real picture. Therefore, the Spirit of the Lord met Gideon, not at church, but at the place where Gideon was functioning out of purpose. He did this so that Gideon could see that he was doing something he had no business doing—hiding his gift instead of using it—all because he was afraid of the enemy.

How did God give Gideon a new picture of himself? In Judges 6:12, the Lord calls him a mighty warrior. This is interesting because Gideon doesn't have a sword or a shield, neither is he on the battlefield. However, the Lord's picture of Gideon isn't in the present tense. God is showing Gideon a picture of what he's getting ready to do. He says to him, "You mighty warrior." God, who calls things that are not as though they were, has spoken a life-transforming word to Gideon. God's Word always gives a new light and new perspective. Gideon would never be the same. Even though he had not started fighting yet, God is giving him a picture and saying, "See yourself being victorious."

In the very place the enemy thought he had you hemmed in, God has spoken and changed your image and your destiny. Now picture yourself being successful. Picture yourself being victorious. Picture yourself being the head and not the tail. Picture yourself being a four-star general of faith, because you are more than a conqueror. Picturing yourself within the correct contextual frame and having the right image directly affects how you dream and what you dream about. There is nothing wrong with being a dreamer, particularly when you're dreaming according to the plans that God has in store for you. Get ready for it—that big idea is on the way!

Five
DREAMS

When the LORD restored the fortunes of Zion, we were like those who dreamed. Our mouths were filled with laughter, our tongues with songs of joy. Then it was said among the nations, "The LORD has done great things for them." Psalm 126:1-2

Fifty days after our Lord's crucifixion, on the Day of Pentecost, a dramatic shift occurred that changed the landscape of biblical history forever. After Jesus had rose from the dead, the Dispensation of Grace kicked into high gear. Believers of all nations, tribes, and tongues were no longer excluded from the blessings and covenants of promise given exclusively to Israel. Additionally, no longer were believers to be burdened by the strict moral, ethical, and legal statutes of the Law, which had kept people in bondage since the days of Moses. Now, believers had the freedom to stand fast in the liberty of Christ by faith. On this defining day, God flipped the pages of His divine plan that changed two-thousand years of history. He started a completely new chapter called the Church, which was empowered and authenticated by the Holy Spirit.

As was their tradition, the Jews of the Diaspora made their pilgrimage from various countries back to Jerusalem to worship God and celebrate the Day of Pentecost. The environment was charged, particularly because Jesus had been crucified fifty days earlier. To the Jewish leaders, it was a done deal. "Now we can get on with our business, with no more interference and exploits from this rabble-rousing self-proclaimed messiah." They'd accused this radical named Jesus of being a blasphemer and a false prophet. By their own wicked hands, they had set up false witnesses and demanded that he be crucified. However, three days later, Jesus rose from the dead.

During a forty-day period, the Lord appeared to the apostles and instructed them concerning their new mission, which would turn the world upside down. Jesus taught the apostles many things pertaining to the kingdom of God. However, before He was taken up into heaven, He commanded them to go to Jerusalem and wait for the gift from the Father—the baptism of the Holy Spirit. In obedience to the Lord, they left the Mount of Olives and traveled about a day's journey to Jerusalem. They found lodging in the upper room, where they waited (tarried) for the Holy Spirit.

In Acts 1: 8, Jesus said to his apostles, "But you will receive power when the Holy Spirit comes on you; and you will be my witnesses in Jerusalem, and in all Judea and Samaria, and to the ends of the earth." Witnesses are living proof that Jesus and His message are alive and well forevermore. When the Holy Spirit was poured out on the Day of Pentecost, Peter spoke the most anointed message ever preached in the annals of Church history. Two thousand people gave their lives to Christ, and the age of the Church began.

In Acts 2 verses 1 through 4, we have the account of what happened when the Holy Spirit fell. A "rushing mighty wind" of the Spirit, along with "tongues of fire," rested on each of the one hundred and twenty or so people in the upper room that day. Immediately, they all began to speak with other tongues as the Spirit enabled them. Apparently, this caused a great commotion because those outside the establishment could hear what was going on in the upper room. This twofold miracle enabled those in the upper room to speak in a supernatural heavenly language that the hearers understood in their own native tongues. There were Jews from at least fifteen nations (with as many dialects) present that day. This miracle was so amazing that those gathered there asked, "Aren't all these who are speaking Galileans? Then how is it that each of us hears them in our native language?"

Immediately, the enemy began to attack the validity of this miracle-message by claiming that the people in the upper room were drunk. However, Peter, under the unction of the Holy Spirit, used simple apologetic wit and reasoning to preach to the people that what they were witnessing was not the result of copious libation, but the fulfillment of Old Testament prophecy. Here is what Peter said,

"…Fellow Jews and all of you who live in Jerusalem, let me explain this to you; listen carefully to what I say. These people are not drunk, as you suppose. It's only nine in the morning! No, this is what was spoken by the prophet Joel: "'In the last days, God says, I will pour out my Spirit on all people. Your sons and daughters will prophesy, your young men will see visions, your old men will dream dreams. Even on my servants, both men and women, I will pour out my Spirit in those days, and they will prophesy.'"

Acts 2:14-18

Here, Peter announced a new age of believers that would have the gifts to prophesy, see visions, and dream dreams, all enabled by the indwelling of the Holy Spirit.

ANATOMY OF A DREAM

What is a dream? According to *The American Heritage Dictionary*, a dream is defined as: 1) a series of images, ideas, emotions, and sensations occurring involuntarily in the mind during certain stages of sleep; 2) a daydream; a reverie; 3) a state of abstraction; a trance; 4) a wild fancy or hope; 5) a condition or achievement that is longed for; an aspiration. In the *Zondervan Pictorial Encyclopedia of the Bible*, the late Dr. James Lower, a former professor at Wheaton College, gives the following psychological definition:

> Dreams are the reappearance of thoughts formed in our minds, being portions of previous conceptions and/or impressions revived and randomly reassembled, and are a link between sensation and memory. Dreams are constructed around what we've seen and said, and are based upon memory images collected and preserved in the unconscious since earliest childhood.

In Sigmund Freud's book, *The Interpretation of Dreams*, he espoused a theory that nothing we do occurs by chance; every action and thought is motivated by our unconscious at some level. In order to live in a civilized society, we have a tendency to hold back our urges and repress our impulses. However, these urges and impulses must be released in some way. They have a way of coming to the surface, disguised in the form of dreams.

Though many psychoanalysts do not accept all of Freud's explanation for dreams today, all would agree that there are some interesting facts about dreams. 1) Dreams occur typically during the rapid eye movement stage (REM), which is a deep level of sleep. 2) Most think that during sleep, the brain is less active. However, during sleep, the brain has more activity. 3) Some people often claim they don't dream. However, research proves that we always dream but we don't always recall the dreams. 4) The average person dreams between one and two hours per night, and has as many as seven dreams. 5) During REM sleep, your eyes continue to move, but your body experiences a level of paralysis that some researchers believe helps prevent us from physically acting out during the dreams. According to the research conducted at the University of Toronto, neuroscientists Patricia L. Brooks and John H. Peever, Ph.D., found that certain neurotransmitters caused REM sleep paralysis by "switching off" the specialized cells in the brain that allow muscles to be active. Those who have REM sleep disorder still have movement during this stage and can seriously injure themselves or others around them.

Big Ideas In Dreams

The idea for many great and revolutionary inventions have come from dreams. Madam C. J. Walker, an African American woman, is recorded by *Guinness Book of World Records* as the *first* American woman to become a self-made millionaire. Madam Walker, the first member of her family to be born free (1867), suffered from a nagging scalp infection. She prayed to God about her condition, and He answered the prayer in a dream, giving her the big idea for a cream to cure scalp infection. She started a company and began manufacturing her products, becoming a millionaire several times over. Other big ideas for discoveries, inventions, and creativity that came through dreams are Albert Einstein's theory of relativity, Larry Page's idea for Google, Nikola Tesla's idea for the alternating current (AC) generator, Frederick Banting's discovery of insulin for the treatment of diabetes, and the melody for the most re-recorded song in history, Paul McCartney's classic *Yesterday*, came to him in a dream.

Another strange phenomenon about dreams is that some people have even dreamed about their own death. Such was the case with eighteen-year-old Michael Brown of Ferguson, Missouri. On the morning of August 9, 2014, Michael, unarmed and according to witnesses, was surrendering to police with his hands up, was shot by a Ferguson police officer. With numerous witnesses looking on in horror and disbelief, Michael was shot multiple times in cold blood. The public outcry against the unwarranted murder was immediate.

In the aftermath of this shooting riots reminiscent of those that followed the assassination of Dr. Martin Luther King, Jr. ensued as police in riot gear, carrying assault rifles and driving armored tanks, fired tear gas grenades and rubber bullets at angry protesters. News outlets all over the world covered this tragic story and even blasted the U.S. for its hypocrisy on human rights. President Barack Obama called for peace in the wake of the unrest in Ferguson. He also dispatched United States Attorney General Eric Holder to Ferguson to launch a thorough federal investigation.

On August 26, at the funeral services for Michael Brown, his stepmother, Cal Brown, told of Michael's dreams where he prophesied about his own death. Mrs. Brown told thousands of grieving mourners how after she had been released from the hospital after surgery, she had a heart-to-heart talk with "Mike Mike" (as she called him). In their conversation, he told her "he didn't think she was going to make it after her surgical procedure." After asking him why he thought that, Michael told her that lately he had been having a lot of dreams about death. "I see pictures of death. I see pictures of bloody sheets hanging from a clothes line." Cal Brown went on to say that on that unforgettable tragic morning, she went out and saw his lifeless body lying on the street, under a bloody sheet. Mike Mike also told her, "One day the world is going to know my name," and "He is going to shake the world." Regrettably, it all came to pass on a Saturday morning in Ferguson, Missouri.

NATURAL DREAMS

In the Bible, the word "dream" in its various forms is found over one hundred times. However, in the New Testament, the word only appears seven times. Six are found in Matthew and are in reference to Jesus, and one is in Acts, where the word is quoted from Joel 2:28. Dreams can be categorized in three ways: natural, divine, and evil.

In Ecclesiastes 5:3a KJV, Solomon says this about dreams: "For a dream cometh through the multitude of business." Here the Bible speaks briefly of dreams in the natural course of life. The implication is that the more affairs (experiences) we have in life, the more we have to dream about. Solomon's assessment of dreams goes back to the very premises that dreams are a collection of memory images from our life's experiences. Whether good or bad, joyous or sad, dreams are boundless, without regard to the constraints of logic, the restraint of reason or the bounds of physical laws or ability. Whether whimsical or terrifying, the mind freely associates and reassembles our experience stimuli in the form of a dream. Dreams are fed by our deepest emotions, passions, desires, and fears. As some have described it, dreams are the gatekeepers of our sleep.

Another example of natural dreams occurs when physical needs inspire the dream. In Isaiah 29:7-8, the prophet says,

> … as it is with a dream, with a vision in the night— as when a hungry person dreams of eating, but awakens hungry still; as when a thirsty person dreams of drinking, but awakens faint and thirsty still.

Contextually, the prophet is comparing Sennacherib's army's disappointment to a hungry person whose hunger and thirst inspire dreams of eating and drinking, only to awaken to the reality of having neither. Our hopes and desires can inspire dreams, whether or not there is any basis for them coming to pass.

DIVINE DREAMS

The Bible also speaks of dreams that God gives in order to instruct and direct people. These are divine dreams. In Numbers 12:6, the Lord says, "Listen to my words: "When there is a prophet among you, I, the LORD, reveal myself to them in visions, I speak to them in dreams." Here, God informs us concerning the way He typically chooses to speak to his prophets. In Genesis 28:11-14, we have the account of Jacob's ladder, where God informs Jacob about the blessedness of his posterity.

> When he reached a certain place, he stopped for the night because the sun had set. Taking one of the stones there, he put it under his head and lay down to sleep. He had a dream in which he saw a stairway resting on the earth, with its top reaching to heaven, and the angels of God were ascending and descending on it. There above it stood the LORD, and he said: "I am the LORD, the God of your father Abraham and the God of Isaac. I will give you and your descendants the land on which you are lying. Your descendants will be like the dust of the earth, and you will spread out to the west and to the east, to the north and to the south. All peoples on earth will be blessed through you and your offspring.

Another example of a divine dream is when God uses the dream to turn us from sin or to steer us away from destruction. In Job 33:14-17, we read,

> For God speaks, the first time in one way, the second time in another, though a person does not perceive it. In a dream, a night vision, when deep sleep falls on people as they sleep in their beds. Then he gives a revelation to people, and terrifies them with warnings, to turn a person from his sin, and to cover a person's pride. (NET)

Examples of God warning in dreams are found in Genesis 20:3, where God warned Abimelech not to touch Abraham's wife. In Matthew 2:12, the wise men were warned not to return to Herod. And concerning Jesus's trial, Pilate's wife complained of suffering "a great deal today in a dream because of him," and warned her husband not to have anything to do with Him. In these instances, God gave divine dreams for instruction and direction.

Prophetic Dreams

The prophetic dreams are those dreams that serve a foretelling function and focus on events that will come to pass in the relatively short future, or will be fulfilled hundreds and even thousands of years later. One of the greatest examples of a prophetic dream in the Old Testament is found in the story of Joseph. In Genesis 37:5-11 KJV, Joseph was a dreamer.

> And Joseph dreamed a dream, and he told it his brethren: and they hated him yet the more. And he said unto them, Hear, I pray you, this dream which I have dreamed: For, behold, we were binding sheaves in the field, and, lo, my sheaf arose, and also stood upright; and, behold, your sheaves stood round about, and made obeisance to my sheaf. And his brethren said to him, Shalt thou indeed reign over us? or shalt thou indeed have dominion over us? And they hated him yet the more for his dreams, and for his words. And he dreamed yet another dream, and told it his brethren, and said, Behold, I have dreamed a dream more; and, behold, the sun and the moon and the eleven stars made obeisance to me. And he told it to his father, and to his brethren: and his father rebuked him, and said unto him, What is this dream that thou hast dreamed? Shall I and thy mother and thy brethren indeed come to bow

down ourselves to thee to the earth? And his brethren envied him; but his father observed the saying.

Joseph was only seventeen years old when he had those two prophetic dreams. Though Joseph didn't understand the meaning of his dreams, they were divine prophecies given by God concerning Joseph's future role in saving his family and the nation of Israel. The one aspect of both dreams that everyone did understand is that according to the dreams, they were all going to bow before Joseph. That idea was not well received. In the upcoming chapters, we will take a closer examination into the mistakes that dreamers often make.

The Interpretation of Dreams

Dreams by nature are very abstract, stringing together thoughts, imaginations, experiences, and desires into fantastical, vivid imagery and vignettes that are often difficult to interpret. In the vast majority of incidences, dreams are completely meaningless and are nothing more than a mere exercise of the subconscious that has no impact on reality. Therefore, one must be very cautious in attempting to extract meaning or attempting to assign relevance to every dream. Whereas some aspects of one's dream may be real—as one may dream about a real job or a real person—the dream about that job or person may have no meaning in reality. In your dream, you may see yourself flying a passenger jet, but in reality, you are a sixty-year-old school bus driver who'll never have a chance at flying a commercial airliner. To walk away with the interpretation that it's time to make a career change to piloting based on that dream would be a serious mistake.

Each year, millions of dollars are spent on the interpretation of dreams. There are dream dictionaries, psychics, astrologers, and a host of other persons, places, and things all set up to take your money. These all fall into the category of evil dreams. Here's what the Lord has to say regarding evil dreams and dreamers.

> "I have heard what the prophets say who prophesy lies in my name. They say, 'I had a dream! I had a dream!' Yes, this is what the LORD Almighty, the God of Israel, says: "Do not let the prophets and diviners among you deceive you. Do not listen to the dreams you encourage them to have. They are prophesying lies to you in my name. I have not sent them," declares the LORD.

Jeremiah 23:25, 29:8-9

These passages are clear. False dreamers feed into the hopes and desires of people that have turned to them for guidance. Then, the false prophet reciprocates with dreams that coincide with what those fool-hearted people want to hear, thereby perpetuating a cycle of deception. However, this is not the case with the divine dream. In Genesis 40, Joseph's story continues. He has already gone through many terrible incidents. His brothers sold him into slavery. He was falsely accused of rape by Potiphar's wife and thrown into prison. After years of being in prison, two men from Pharaoh's court were locked up where Joseph is held. One day Joseph sees these men's sad countenances and inquires about what's troubling them. Here's what the text says next, "We both had dreams," they answered, "but there is no one to interpret them." Then Joseph said to them, "Do not interpretations belong to God? Tell me your dreams" (Verse 8).

Joseph has made the most important point as it relates to the interpretation of dreams—interpretation of dreams belongs to God. Only God knows our thoughts before we even think them and knows our dreams before we dream them.

Another example of divine dream interpretation is found in Daniel 2. In verses 1-4 and 8-10, Daniel interprets a dream that was forgotten by King Nebuchadnezzar.

> In the second year of his reign, Nebuchadnezzar had dreams; his mind was troubled and he could not sleep. So the king summoned the magicians, enchanters, sorcerers and astrologers to tell him what he had dreamed. When they came in and stood before the king, he said to them, "I have had a dream that troubles me and I want to know what it means." Then the astrologers answered the king, "May the king live forever! Tell your servants the dream, and we will interpret it."
>
> Then the king answered, "I am certain that you are trying to gain time, because you realize that this is what I have firmly decided: If you do not tell me the dream, there is only one penalty for you. You have conspired to tell me misleading and wicked things, hoping the situation will change. So then, tell me the dream, and I will know that you can interpret it for me." The astrologers answered the king, "There is no one on earth who can do what the king asks!

In these verses, we find that after King Nebuchadnezzar had his dream, he summoned his mystic cabinet of magicians, enchanters, sorcerers, and astrologers. All of these mystical arts fall under the broad banner of *divination*. Divination is the practice of consulting beings—whether spiritual, human or departed—or things, by the observation of objects or actions, in an attempt to gain information about the future and such matters that are removed from normal knowledge. Divination is related to magic, but is distinct from it in mainly in that the latter attempts to produce a certain effect, while the former seeks knowledge. In either case, the practice was strictly forbidden amongst God's people (Deuteronomy 18:10, 14).

After the word reached Daniel about the king's plan to kill all the prophets, Daniel and the three Hebrew boys (Hananiah, Mishael and Azariah) sought the Lord in an all-night prayer meeting to petition God to recover the lost dream. That's when God revealed the dream to Daniel. In response, here are the praises Daniel rendered to the Lord.

> …Then Daniel praised the God of heaven and said: "Praise be to the name of God for ever and ever; wisdom and power are his. He changes times and seasons; he deposes kings and raises up others. He gives wisdom to the wise and knowledge to the discerning. He reveals deep and hidden things; he knows what lies in darkness, and light dwells with him. I thank and praise you, God of my ancestors: You have given me wisdom and power, you have made known to me what we asked of you, you have made known to us the dream of the king."
>
> Daniel 2:19-23

What we must walk away with from this is the fact that God is the giver of the divine dream, and He is the only interpreter of dreams. There is no witch, warlock, astrologer, tarot card or palm reader that can reveal dreams or that knows what tomorrow brings. No one but God!

THE TRANCE

Closely related to dreams are trances and visions. According *The American Heritage Dictionary*, a trance is: 1) a hypnotic, cataleptic, or ecstatic state; 2) detachment from one's physical surroundings, as in contemplation or daydreaming; 3) a semi-conscious state, as between sleeping and waking; a daze. In the King James Version of the Bible, the word trance is found five times. The two incidents where it's found in the Old Testament are both in Numbers 24, verses 4 and 16, where the translators inserted the word. Additionally, it's found in the New Testament only three times: Acts 10:10, 11:5, 22:17, where the Greek word is *ekstasis* (ek-sta-sis). Ekstasis comes from a word that means "displacement of the mind, i.e. bewilderment, ecstasy." Trances are different from dreams in that the recipient maintains some level of consciousness. An example of this is found in Numbers 24:4 where it says, "He hath said, which heard the words of God, which saw the vision of the Almighty, falling into a trance, but having his eyes open."

In Acts 10:10, Peter was in prayer on a rooftop when he fell into a trance and God gave him a vision of a great sheet coming down from heaven with several different types of ceremonially unclean animals. Peter then heard God's voice command him to "kill and eat." The vision was in relationship to Peter having to open the doors of the Church to the Gentiles, who by Mosaic Law, were considered as unclean and were not to partake in the blessing and common wealth of Israel. Here the trance, instead of unconscious sleep, was the state of mind that allowed the receiver to see the vision.

The Vision

One of the most quoted passages of scripture containing the word "vision" is found in Proverbs 29:18 KJV, where is says, "Where there is no vision, the people perish." In other Bible versions, the word is also translated "revelation." In English, the word vision is normally attributed to the ability to see with the natural eyes. However, a divine vision is supernatural, where the seer is not seeing anything physical, but that which comes only by revelation in those dimensions that are extra-physical. Visions are a way God often reveals His instructions and plans, and/or gives His prophets access into His supernatural realm. Apocalyptic books like Ezekiel, Daniel, and Revelation usually contain much vision/revelation material. Typically thematic in apocalyptic literature are the words, "I saw," which occur thirty-six times in the book of Revelation.

Whether it's by dreams, revelation, trances, or through the imagination, God chooses the modus operandi through which He will reveal His divine plans. Whether it is to nations, people, or individuals, God's Word shall not return unto Him void, but it goes out to accomplish that which God has purposed it to do. That means that God not only fulfills biblical promises, but God will fulfill all of the promises that He has made concerning you. God will speak to your heart and give you an awesome dream, a divine revelation to lead you to your destiny.

Six
THE DESIRES OF YOUR HEART

Delight yourself also in the LORD, And He shall give you the
desires of your heart. Commit your way to the LORD, Trust also in
Him, And He shall bring it to pass.
Psalm 37:4-5 NKJV

ecently, *News One Now* host Roland Martin asked callers
to weigh in on whether R&B star Pharrell Williams's
hit song *Happy* should also be sung in churches. As you could
imagine, there were spirited responses on both sides of the issue. Those who were for church choirs singing this song touted
that the song's message and beat were so uplifting that it coincides with the church's mission in bringing happiness to their
congregations. Others who opposed this idea stated that they
felt it was inappropriate for an R&B pop song to be sung in
the context of worshiping God. In hearing both sides of the
issue, it brought up an interesting question. Is it the church's
or God's purpose to make people happy?

Considering all of the challenges we face in life, and the various vicissitudes we encounter, fulfilling our deepest desires in the pursuit of happiness continues to be a high priority. In clinical studies, people were asked what they wanted most out of life. Though there were many answers, the responses boiled down to the following ten most desired things. *Having love in their lives; being healthy; having high-paying jobs; looking better; losing weight and toning their bodies; learning new things; living longer with their families; being safe from perceived and real hurt, harm, and danger; being comfortable; and having more pleasure to satisfy their appetite and desires.* According to the survey, if one achieves the things on the list, they would consider themselves to be happy.

However, let's reframe the question a bit and make it more compatible to the portrait of a Christian. Would you ask for something to make you happy, if you had one opportunity to ask God for anything that you wanted? Would you ask for money and material possessions? Would you ask for popularity or fame? Would you ask to get some payback for those who wronged you? Would you ask God to silence all of your haters? Would you ask for promotion and prestige? Would you ask for more years added to your life? If you were in God's presence and had His undivided attention, what would you ask Him for? While you're contemplating your answer, let's take a look at someone who was in that very position—King Solomon.

SOLOMON'S DREAM

Among the great dream stories in the Bible, King Solomon's dream is one of the greatest, not because of its prophetic value, but because of its content. The account of Solomon's dream is found in 1 Kings 3. This is one of the most phenomenal interactions between God and an individual recorded in the Bible. The text reads as follows,

> The king went to Gibeon to offer sacrifices, for that was the most important high place, and Solomon offered a thousand burnt offerings on that altar. At Gibeon the LORD appeared to Solomon during the night in a dream, and God said, "Ask for whatever you want me to give you."
>
> 1 Kings 3:4-5

Imagine that! God shows up in your dream, and He gives you the opportunity to ask Him for whatever your heart desires. I can almost hear your enthusiasm as you contemplate what would be on your goodies list. "God, I have always wanted this. Lord, I just have to have that," and on and on. However, Solomon didn't do that. As a matter of fact, he did just the opposite, with stunning results. Here's how Solomon replied.

> "Now, LORD my God, you have made your servant king in place of my father David. But I am only a little child and do not know how to carry out my duties. Your servant is here among the people you have chosen, a great people, too numerous to count or number. So give your servant a discerning heart to govern your people and to distinguish between right and wrong. For who is able to govern this great people of yours?"
>
> 1 Kings 3:7-9

We can learn a great deal from Solomon's response. First of all, what's missing here? Is there any mention of wealth, life, revenge, promotion, elimination of enemies? No, none of that. Solomon stays focused on his God-given purpose. Solomon was Israel's third king and everything he asked God for was pertaining to what God called him to do. Secondly, Solomon exhibited humility when he confessed his inability to carry out the task of being king on his own. Thirdly, and probably most importantly, Solomon used the word "I" only once, but used "you" and "your" six times, referring to God. Without a doubt, Solomon understood whose plan was to be fulfilled and whose agenda was to be followed—God's, not his.

God's amazing response is recorded in verses 10 through 15.

The Lord was pleased that Solomon had asked for this. So God said to him, "Since you have asked for this and not for long life or wealth for yourself, nor have asked for the death of your enemies but for discernment in administering justice, I will do what you have asked. I will give you a wise and discerning heart, so that there will never have been anyone like you, nor will there ever be. Moreover, I will give you what you have not asked for—both wealth and honor—so that in your lifetime you will have no equal among kings. And if you walk in obedience to me and keep my decrees and commands as David your father did, I will give you a long life." Then Solomon awoke—and he realized it had been a dream.

God's response is off the charts! God says, since you have asked how to be exceptional at fulfilling my purpose for your life, and not for small stuff like money or material things, I will give you much more than what you asked for—over the top unparalleled wisdom. And I will give you what you *didn't* ask for—over the top and unparalleled honor and wealth greater than any other king. The icing on the cake was when God said, "In your lifetime you will have no equal among kings." God set Solomon far and above all the other kings on the earth in riches, wisdom, and honor. Solomon was wise enough not to waste time asking for trivial things while in the presence of the Almighty God.

I once heard the story of a young federal correctional officer who worked at the Metropolitan Correction Center in downtown Chicago. He was having a conversation with a convicted mafia boss. The wise guy told him, "If you ever get the chance to go before someone great, never make a small request." In other words "Don't disrespect access to greatness with a trivial matter or request." If you have the honor to have an audience with the President of the United States, don't go to him with a frivolous matter; honor that access with a request that only the President can do.

We are kingdom kids. We are the Master's children. In Christ, we have inherited all things according to His riches in glory. It's already yours! This is why Jesus said your heavenly Father already knows what you need before you ask Him, but seek ye first the kingdom of God and all its righteousness, then the things will be added. Jesus is saying we should have a heavenly perspective and kingdom mentality. You should be walking in the full knowledge and authority of your purpose and make your calling and election sure. So when you come before His presence with thanksgiving and enter His courts with praise, you don't dishonor Him by asking God to do something your cousin can do. However, honor God by asking for the ability to fulfill His purpose for your life. Inside your purpose will be all of the provision for your life as we see with Solomon. Have the mindset of David, who said, "One thing have I desired of the LORD, that will I seek after; that I may dwell in the house of the LORD all the days of my life, to behold the beauty of the LORD, and to enquire in his temple" (Psalm 27:4 KJV). When you are in God's presence, desire the right thing!

In Ephesians 3:20, we have this great doxology, "Now to him who is able to do immeasurably more than all we ask or imagine, according to his power that is at work within us." Solomon accessed the "immeasurably" more level of blessing from God. This is a level of blessing that you cannot ask or imagine because it's beyond your capacity to even conceive. This level of blessing is not according to what you can ask, but it is according to the power that works within you. God knows what His plans are for you, but you don't know until He reveals them to you. That's why we must wait upon the Lord, not with inactivity, but with anticipation as we work to better ourselves. The power that works within you encompasses those plans and purposes that God has placed in you. However, it is your responsibility to work them out.

WHOSE DESIRE, WHOSE PLAN

In Jeremiah 29:11, there's a great passage of scripture that's often preached to encourage people that are in the midst of a fiery trial. The passage reads, "For I know the plans I have for you," declares the LORD, "plans to prosper you and not to harm you, plans to give you hope and a future." However, when that passage is preached, it's usually taken out of context and used as a passage of exhortation. But in its historical-grammatical context, the passage takes on even greater significance. Jeremiah 29 is really a letter that Jeremiah has sent to the Jews that have been taken captive into Babylon. Here's how the letter begins.

> This is what the LORD Almighty, the God of Israel, says to all
> those I carried into exile from Jerusalem to Babylon: "Build
> houses and settle down; plant gardens and eat what they pro-
> duce. Marry and have sons and daughters; find wives for your
> sons and give your daughters in marriage, so that they too may
> have sons and daughters. Increase in number there; do not de-
> crease. Also, seek the peace and prosperity of the city to which
> I have carried you into exile. Pray to the LORD for it, because
> if it prospers, you too will prosper." Yes, this is what the LORD
> Almighty, the God of Israel, says: "Do not let the prophets and
> diviners among you deceive you. Do not listen to the dreams
> you encourage them to have. They are prophesying lies to you
> in my name.

Jeremiah 29:5-8

Here we see that Israel has been taken into captivity by the
Babylonians (modern day Iraq). However, God's instructions
are: settle down, dig in for the long haul (seventy years), let
your sons and daughters marry, start-up businesses (plant vine-
yards), pray for the prosperity of the city so that you may prosper as it prospers, increase in number, and do not decrease,
(don't kill yourselves, commit suicide or have abortions).

The reason why Jeremiah's letter was necessary is that there
were conflicting messages coming within Israel from false
prophets who were influencing the people to follow their lying
dreams. The false dreamers were probably saying, "This is not
the will of God that we are in captivity. Let's rise up against the
enemy. God will rescue us shortly. Help is on the way. Don't get
involved in politics or start up any businesses because we're not
going to be here long. It's better not to have children than to

let them be born as captives." Unfortunately, too many people were being deceived, so God sent a word through Jeremiah to tell His people what God's plan for them was. God said these words, "For I know the plans I have for you...." That's the primary point of Jeremiah's letter, to convey to the Jews and to us today, that no matter how difficult what you are going through is, God has a good plan for your life. However, many of us are not hearing God's plan because we're too busy following those who the enemy sends to whisper into our ears. The question is, which is the best plan for your life? Yours, theirs, or God's?

We opened this chapter with a quote from Psalm 37:4, which says, "Delight yourself also in the LORD, And He shall give you the desires of your heart." When God says that He will give you the desires of your heart, does this mean any desire applies and no matter how extravagant or frivolous, God is obligated to give it? What about things that are not according to His will for your life? Though most interpret this passage to mean that God is responding to *your* desires, I would like to pose an additional rendering of this passage.

This passage can be understood to mean that God *gives to you* or initiates the desires of your heart. In other words, God gives to you the desire itself, not just the object of your desire. For example, if God has called you to be a pastor, He starts fulfilling that in you with a desire to be a pastor. In this case, the desire originates with God. It becomes *their* desire after God has imparted it to them. However, we can also take comfort in the fact that God also knows our heart's delights and responds to those desires gratuitously, just as our earthly parents delight in giving their children the things they desire, like toys. Those are the "just because I love you gifts," that are not necessarily purpose related.

If we focus on the first way to interpret the passage, "…give you the desires of *your heart*," then God is responding to desires that originate within you. We learned earlier that *natural dreams* are inspired by our own desires. These desires are based upon the things you want in life, in accordance with your goals and aspirations. Your desires are also influenced by all of the stimuli and messaging that you get from all the various sources of information that enter through your sensory gates. Your desires are either encouraged or discouraged by whose voice you hear and obey. Whose report you receive and believe affects what desires you will have and what dreams you will dream. However, the wrong dreams will have a devastating effect on the outcomes of your life. Wrong messaging leads to wrong desires. Wrong desires lead to wrong dreams. Wrong dreams lead to the wrong direction. The wrong direction leads to the wrong destination.

THE GOD-GIVEN DREAM

Let's examine an alternative way to understand this passage just by placing the emphasis on *He shall give you…*. The phrase "he shall give you" comes from the Hebrew word *nathan* (naw-than) and can be translated several ways, but a few are: *put, give, grant, cause, and deliver*. When you place the emphasis here, it renders "*God gives to you* the desires of your heart." When we interpret the passage this way, it's God who imparts desires to you and it's these desires that He's ultimately bringing to pass. Therefore, it's really Him working through you.

However, God goes further than the desires. He also gives the gifts and enablements to bring to pass the very things He has called you to do. God places within you His plans, which are downloaded from the Holy Spirit to your spirit and soul, and which manifest consciously as things you desire. Therefore, His desires become your desires. As you commit your way (life) to Him, He will bring it to pass. God does this because He knows the plans that He has for you. It's His design to bring you to an expected end. It's not happenstance, a mere circumstance, or lucky stars, but it's God's divine dream that He imparts to you to fulfill His will for your life. This is why the Bible also informs us, "The steps of a good man are ordered by the LORD" (Psalm 37:23).

Your desires and dreams are all in response to His divine purpose and plan for your life. No matter what you've been through in life, no matter how bad it was, or how bad you were, if your heart is pumping and you're breathing air, God has a purpose and a plan for your life. You're nobody's accident. You have a God-given purpose and a God-given dream to fulfill. This is why the devil has set hell on your doorstep. But God is going to make all of your troubles work out for your good, according to His purpose. It's why the devil hates so intensely. Every trap he has laid to destroy you, God turns around and uses the same thing to make you better and bless you. It's the ultimate smack in the devils face. You have an unfair advantage—God's favor!

TO WILL AND TO DO

In Philippians 2:13, we find this powerful word. "For it is God which worketh in you both to will and to do of his good pleasure" (KJV). In this power-packed passage, we learn some great truths about God's sovereign role in our life. It is God who is working His plans through our lives. He places His purpose within us, but we have the responsibility and task of working it out. One of the ways He does this is through imagination, desire, and dreams. For example, in Genesis 15, we see God engaging Abraham's imagination when He tells him about the nation that would proceed from him.

> He took him outside and said, "Look up at the sky and count the stars—if indeed you can count them." Then he said to him, "So shall your offspring be." Abram believed the LORD, and he credited it to him as righteousness. He also said to him, "I am the LORD, who brought you out of Ur of the Chaldeans to give you this land to take possession of it."
>
> Verses 5-7

There are three key elements to be examined in this passage. The first one is that God told Abraham, "Look up at the sky and count the stars." God is giving Abraham a visual aid to engage his imagination. From that point on, God's plan for Abraham's life had been imprinted upon Abraham's imagination. Whenever he looked into the expansive night sky and beheld the beauty and multiplicity of the galaxies and constellations, he would connect that to God's awesome promise and plan for his life.

Secondly, the passage informs us that once God told Abraham about His plans and gave him a photocopy for his imagination to focus on, the Bible says that, "Abram believed the

Lord, and he credited it to him as righteousness." Here we clearly see the substance of faith being activated in Abraham's life, which immediately produced the fruit of righteousness. God counted Abraham's faith as righteousness. This sets the foundation for the doctrine of justification by faith that is thematically taught by the apostle Paul in New Testament epistles. In Hebrews 11:6, the Scriptures inform us that "without faith it is impossible to please God." Therefore, God provided Abraham with a plan for his life and his posterity, set up the visual mechanism for his imagination to engage his faith, and gave him righteousness based upon his belief.

Thirdly, God told Abraham, "I am the Lord, who brought you out of Ur of the Chaldeans to give you this land to take possession of it." There is no controversy here. God said, "I am the one who is doing this," making Himself clear so that none of us ever gets this point confused. He said you're doing what I want you do according to the plans that I have, not only for you and Sarah, but for an entire nation, the entire world, and for my eternal kingdom. God's immediate agenda concerned Abraham, but most of God's purpose for Abraham was much bigger than Abraham's and Sarah's baby. The salient point here is the purpose and the dream that God gives to you is not just about you but it is much bigger than you. These are truly the "big ideas."

As we return to our Philippians text, there are two important elements to this passage that require examination: "to will" and "to do." To "will" is the desire to do something. It is our volition, our hopes, our dreams. These very hopes and dreams are attached to the very gifts, callings, and talents that God gives to us. Sometimes, our gifts become evident from the earliest years of our life. It's the stuff we're born with it. For example, some children are born musically inclined and desire to play an instrument or sing. They didn't learn it from anyone. They're born with the ability to express themselves musically. They come into this world with the innate imagination and creativity to play an instrument or even compose music. Such was the case with the child prodigy Mozart, who was composing classical pieces at age five. Mozart would have been as any other five-year-old child had not God given him this extraordinary ability.

It is important to note that the "will" or the desire to do something is not enough. Desire alone will not bring anything to pass. "To will" must also be accompanied by the ability "to do." As in the case with Abraham, he and Sarah desired to have children, but there was a natural inability for Sarah to conceive. Therefore, desire was not enough. However, we know that it was God who opened up Sarah's womb and superseded Abraham's impotence, to give them both the ability "to do," to fulfill God's plan. In order for a septuagenarian (a person in their nineties) and an octogenarian (a person in their eighties) to reproduce, God stepped into the physical realm and overrode natural inability. He miraculously gave ability to a dead womb to bear a miracle child, so that He would be glorified by bringing to pass the promises that He swore to Abraham.

The desire to do it, and the ability to do it, both came from God. From this, we see that God gives us the *mind* "to will" and the *power* "to do" His good pleasure. God doesn't do the work for us. Abraham and Sarah had to come together in intimacy in order to produce that child. That wasn't God's part—that was their part. In order for us to bring forth our God-given dreams, we must have the faith to act. Even when it seems impossible to us, nothing is impossible with God.

Seven
PERFECTING THE DREAM

We all know that dreams can range from being very vivid, with sharp details and images, to being very obscure vignettes of fantastical, mystical, and sometimes even terrifying images. They're like short films of the mind. In many of our dreams, one character may be transposed onto another because the subconscious mind doesn't seem to concern itself with getting all the details right. A dream about your brother or sister may actually have your uncle or aunt in that role. It's for reasons like this that we must be ever cautious in acting on information received from a dream.

However, when it comes to God-given dreams, they're like seeds planted in your spirit. Just as it takes time for an apple seed to become a fruit-bearing tree, it also takes time for a God-given dream to come to fulfillment. Attempting to help a dream come true before its time has led many people into peril. Though you're the custodian of the dream, we're resigned to waiting on God to bring all of the right conditions together to fulfill it. In many cases, the dream is inherently bigger than you, which means there are others who will be impacted and/ or influenced by you fulfilling your dreams.

In the previous chapter, we discovered that God gave Abraham a visual reference that engaged his imagination. Once Abraham was told he was going to be the father of many nations and would inherit much land, Abraham asked God, "How shall I know this thing shall come to pass?" God responded to Abraham's inquiry with some specific instructions.

> But Abram said, "Sovereign LORD, how can I know that I will gain possession of it?" So the LORD said to him, "Bring me a heifer, a goat and a ram, each three years old, along with a dove and a young pigeon." Abram brought all these to him, cut them in two and arranged the halves opposite each other; the birds, however, he did not cut in half. Then birds of prey came down on the carcasses, but Abram drove them away.
>
> Genesis 15:8-10

Here we see that God instructs Abraham to bring items typically used in a sacrificial offering. However, once Abraham prepared the animals, the passage tells us that birds of prey came to steal the sacrifices, and Abraham had to fight them off. Here, the birds of prey represent the enemy coming to steal, kill, and to destroy. Ever since Adam abdicated his rulership to the devil in the Garden of Eden, the kingdom of darkness has the agenda to contest the move of God in the earth realm. No matter who you are or what you have set out to do for the kingdom of God, it will be contested by the devil. No one, not even Jesus in His earthly ministry, gets a pass on this one.

The Bible clearly teaches that in this life you shall have tribulation. Even in the face of God's promises, and even though the promises and the victory are already yours, there can be no victory without a battle. Have you ever wondered why you've been receiving so much opposition from the enemy? He's using people and circumstances to discourage and harass you. It's not because you're simply being *picked on*; it's because you have been *picked out* to be the custodian of a God-given dream and a divine purpose. There's an awesome calling on your life, and the devil can't stand it. Your success is an affront to the kingdom of darkness because you're bearing God's image and His light. Your dream is part of His grand plan to defeat the devil. Therefore, Satan is mad as hell and is going to throw everything he can at you to get you to turn back. But the devil is a liar, because greater is He that is in you, than he that is in the world.

Spiritual opposition is a response to a genuine God-given dream. Opposition is any obstruction in the road along the way. Just stay on the road and keep your eyes on the prize, because you are well on the way to fulfilling your dream.

Returning to our text, we see that God reveals His plans to Abraham in a dream.

> As the sun was setting, Abram fell into a deep sleep, and a thick and dreadful darkness came over him. Then the LORD said to him, "Know for certain that for four hundred years your descendants will be strangers in a country not their own and that they will be enslaved and mistreated there. But I will punish the nation they serve as slaves, and afterward they will come out with great possessions. You, however, will go to your ancestors in peace and be buried at a good old age."
>
> Verses 12-15

God downloads His agenda for the Nation of Israel to Abraham hundreds of years in advance. And imagine Abraham beginning to understand the magnitude of his role. He would have that first child to kick off the fulfillment of God's plan. Abraham is eager and ready to get started, but there's one little nagging problem. Abraham and Sarah have no children.

Years went by after God gave Abraham the prophecy and dream, yet there was no child. Therefore Sarah concocted her own plan to have a child by Abraham, using their slave-girl, Hagar, as a surrogate. Abraham agreed to the plan. However, fulfilling the dream that way caused long lasting consequences. When Abraham fathered a child by this other woman, they named him Ishmael. But his birth caused tension in Abraham's house to such a degree that Abraham gave his wife leave to do with the mother of his child as she willed. Sarah treated Hagar so badly that Hagar took Ishmael and fled. But Hagar returned later.

In fulfillment of God's promise, fourteen years later, Sarah has Isaac. But in the subsequent years, as the two boys grow together, the tension between them grows to the point where separation is necessary. To this day, in the Middle East, the lineage of Isaac and the lineage of Ishmael are still in conflict! Ironically, according to the Koran, Ishmael is Abraham's chosen son. However, according to the Bible and Jewish history and tradition, Isaac is Abraham's chosen son because it was through Isaac that God's promises to Abraham were to be fulfilled. All this conflict came about when Sarah decided to help God out to bring the dream to pass.

DON'T KILL THE EGYPTIAN

In the book of Acts, Stephen makes a passionate defense before the Sanhedrin, sighting a long history of Israel's stiff-necked resistance to God. Stephen gives us some insight into Moses's life that we don't find written explicitly in Exodus. In chapter 7, the text reads:

> Moses was educated in all the wisdom of the Egyptians and was powerful in speech and action. "When Moses was forty years old, he decided to visit his own people, the Israelites. He saw one of them being mistreated by an Egyptian, so he went to his defense and avenged him by killing the Egyptian. Moses thought that his own people would realize that God was using him to rescue them, but they did not. The next day Moses came upon two Israelites who were fighting. He tried to reconcile them by saying, 'Men, you are brothers; why do you want to hurt each other?' "But the man who was mistreating the other pushed Moses aside and said, 'Who made you ruler and judge over us? Are you thinking of killing me as you killed the Egyptian yesterday?'
>
> Acts 7:22-28

From this historical narrative, we learn that at about the age of forty, Moses began to identify with his people, the Israelites, who were under cruel slavery in Egypt as was prophesied to Abraham back in Genesis 15. For the first forty years of his life, he had been raised as an Egyptian in Pharaoh's household, receiving the best of everything. He had wealth, status, and the best education. But, at a decisive moment in his life, the dream that he was to be the deliverer came alive in his heart. As the calling of God began to be released in his spirit, I can surmise that Moses began to dream about how he was going to turn things around for his people. I'm sure that Moses saw the people willingly lining up to follow him. He probably dreamed about the day that he would face-off with Pharaoh, the most powerful man in the world. I'm sure that Moses dreamed about restoring all that had been taken from Israel as he advocated for equal rights and justice. Yes, in Moses's dream, the people would recognize him as God's chosen man to lead them to freedom.

However, he was sadly mistaken. Often our callings and dreams become misdirected because we filter them through minds that are confused about who we really are. On one hand, Moses is responding to God's calling, but on the other hand he's executing it through the filter of the Egyptian experience and the dictates of his flesh. The desire to be the deliverer is correct, but the method in bringing that to pass was seriously flawed. That caused him to step into the role before it was time. Killing the Egyptian didn't help his cause, but only made matters worse. Instead of becoming Moses the deliverer, he is now Moses the murderer, who was forced to flee from Pharaoh.

You have a dream that God gives to you according to His divine purposes. It can't be arbitrarily worked out, because the steps have already been ordered. God is the author and the finisher of our faith. Once He begins a work in you, He will complete it. This is why our input, as in the case with Abraham and Moses, can be so disruptive—not to God, but to ourselves. Dreams need to be clarified as we are moving towards fulfillment.

MIXED MESSAGES

Years ago, before iPods, Smartphones, and satellite radio became popular, people often encountered a problem while driving and listening to the radio. The radio signal for the station they were listening to would start to fade, as another radio station's signal got picked up. The next thing you know, you were hearing two different transmissions simultaneously, but unable to understand either. The reason this phenomenon occurred was because as you went out of range of the station you were listening to, the signal weakened. However, as one signal faded out, and you entered the range of another station, that signal began fading in. Midway between both stations' ranges, their signals blended, creating an annoying mixed transmission.

The phenomenon of the fading radio signal is a good analogy of a spiritual truth pertaining to circumstances that affect our dreams. The closer we are to God, the better we can hear His voice. The farther we stray from God, the louder the enemy's voice becomes. The question is, whose report are you receiving and whose report are you ultimately believing? If you're listening to WFAD (the world, the flesh and the devil), your thought and dream life will be impacted by that message. You'll have a lust-based, secularly-conformed mindset and begin to see everything according to the dictates and fashions of the world. In 1 John 2:16, the Scriptures admonishes us, "For everything in the world—the lust of the flesh, the lust of the eyes, and the pride of life—comes not from the Father but from the world." Herein is the problem. Your actions will align with whichever transmission you're receiving. If you entertain the wrong thoughts, you'll have the wrong dreams.

Like the fading radio signals, it becomes difficult to hear from God when we're out of range or out of purpose. While

Moses was in Egypt, he lived, breathed, and thought Egypt. However, once God began to call him out of Egypt, Moses indeed acknowledged the call, but he responded like an Egyptian. But once he got away from Egypt and got in closer proximity to God, he was able to hear directly from the Lord when he entered into His presence at the burning bush. At that decisive moment, Moses was able to step into the role of the deliverer. Without him knowing it, his attempt to fulfill the dream prematurely in the wrong manner was placing the dream in jeopardy.

For us to avoid making some of the same mistakes that Moses made, we need to examine his missteps. If we go back to Acts 7, the first misstep that Moses made is found in verse 23, where it says, "he decided." In Proverbs 3:5-6 we find these words, "Trust in the LORD with all thine heart; and lean not unto thine own understanding. In all thy ways acknowledge him, and he shall direct thy paths" (KJV). Unfortunately, Moses is no different than any other man in regards to us wanting to do things our own way. Pride makes us think that we don't need God. Pride makes us think that we can act independently of Him. Pride gives us an "Invictus" spirit, where we proclaim to be the masters of our own soul. We're not the masters of our own soul, because our souls belong to God and not us (Ezekiel 18:4). The only remedy to this pride problem is to "... acknowledge him, and he shall direct thy paths" (KJV).

The second misstep occurred when Moses went to his fellow Hebrew's defense. Evidently, Moses was feeling himself and his ability to take on his fellow Hebrew's cause. Poor judgment and inexperience will have you picking the wrong battles, where you waste time, energy, and resources, and damage your reputation. Being overconfident can be one of your worst self-inflicted problems. Here's what Paul says about being overconfident: "For by the grace given me I say to every one of you: Do not think of yourself more highly than you ought, but rather think of yourself with sober judgment..." (Romans 12:3 KJV). Exercising humility is the best way to prevent becoming overconfident and haughty. In Philippians Paul also says, that we should "have no confidence in the flesh" (Philippians 3:3). The alternative is not a good one—that's where God puts you on the fast track to humility, like he did with King Nebuchadnezzar. After seven years of having a beast's mind and eating grass like a cow, Nebuchadnezzar learned the hard way to give God the praise. It's better when we humble ourselves rather than having God do it for us.

The third misstep occurs when Moses overacted by killing the Egyptian. Apparently, Moses was dealing with the "hero syndrome." In many families, dysfunctional ones in particular, the oldest child often falls into the role of the "hero" or the "rescuer." This is a "take charge," "step up to the plate" person who takes care of things. They have the answers to everyone's problems. They're the person that everyone in the family turns to. So it becomes an informal role in which they become typecast and form their identity around. They become the one who rescues everyone else, but can't rescue themselves. Heroes take on people as projects and don't feel worthy or secure about themselves unless they have some charity case to manage. In

Moses's case, he reacted prematurely, falsely supposing that he could change things. But the results were deadly. Stepping out there too fast and too soon is highly detrimental, and you will end up killing an Egyptian every time.

Moses's next misstep is that he thought his people would understand his calling and his dream. Usually, we're very wrong on what we suppose people think about us. We often think, "They don't mind. They understand. They like me." We take for granted that we have people's backing, when we don't. People tend not to follow some self-appointed person. God has to authenticate you through His anointing, which comes from you going through trials and tribulations designed to establish and settle you. Unless He places a leadership anointing on you, you won't be able to lead someone across the street. Moses made the mistake of thinking that people would readily follow him and respect him for wanting to change things. He figured; they will understand that I am God's man, here to lead them to the Promised Land. People's allegiance and respect are not something they arbitrarily bandy about. You'd have to had earned their respect. Once you have, it must be cherished because if it's lost, it's difficult—if not impossible—to regain.

The next misstep that Moses made is stepping out with no authority backing him up. The only way to have authority is to be under authority. So when the Hebrew man challenged, "Who made you ruler over us?" Moses had no response. In Matthew 8:8-9 we have the account of the centurion whose servant was at home sick. After he had told Jesus about his servant's condition, the Lord asked, "Shall I come and heal him?"

The centurion replied,

> "Lord, I do not deserve to have you come under my roof. But just say the word, and my servant will be healed. For I myself am a man under authority, with soldiers under me. I tell this one, 'Go,' and he goes; and that one, 'Come,' and he comes. I say to my servant, 'Do this,' and he does it."

The centurion's response amazed Jesus. It sheds light on an important principle about how real authority works. People who are in authority don't need to do anything. They only need to speak, and whatever they say happens. In the boardroom, it's what the chairman says. In the courtroom, it's what the judge says. In the classroom, it's what the teacher says. At home, it's what momma or daddy says. People in authority don't lift a finger, they just open their mouths. When God created the heavens and the earth, He didn't have to go collect stardust to shape the planets. He just spoke! As sons and daughters of God, we also have authority through Christ Jesus to speak to our mountains. But never do what the seven sons of Sceva did in Acts 19 when they tried to cast out a demon from a man. The demon replied, "Jesus I know, and Paul I know, but who are you?" Then he commenced to beating the clothes off of these guys. Never step out there without any authority to back you up.

The final misstep occurred when Moses resorted to violence to carry out his mission. By killing the Egyptian, it undermined his own creditability. The next day after killing the Egyptian, Moses once again interjected himself into another conflict, this time between two Hebrews. However, in attempting to mediate their conflict, one of his fellow Hebrews challenged him by saying, "Are you thinking of killing me as you killed the Egyptian yesterday?" To the Hebrew, Moses had no credibility and didn't deserve his respect because he had resorted to murder. Because of that, the Hebrew felt that Moses was nothing more than a thug who wanted to be a ruler. Insecure individuals who have no authority or respect from others often feel that they have to resort to violence in order to be in control. They think they must gangster their way into everything. Men who physically abuse women often do so because they feel they have no other means of control. The sister may make more money, have more education, and can argue circles around him. He feels that the only way he can win is to beat her up. If the only way you can get a point across is with violence, you will never earn people's respect. If you rule by the sword, you'll die by the sword. But if you ever put down that sword, you'll soon find out how people really feel.

It's never wise to get ahead of God and step out on your own. Remember, your dream is His dream, so let God work out the details. Avoid Abraham's impatience and Moses's missteps and follow the footsteps on the path that has been predestined for you.

Eight
DREAM KILLERS

Up until this point, we've covered many aspects of dreams, from a natural, scientific, and supernatural perspective. However, in this chapter we're changing course to address the situations and circumstances that come to destroy or distract you from achieving your dreams, called dream killers.

Many have incorrectly surmised that if you kill the dreamer, you have killed the dream. The likelihood of that happening is increased considerably if the dream has never been spoken. However, once a dream has been transported from thought into spoken words, it may be difficult to stop. One of the greatest dreamers that the world has ever known was civil rights icon Dr. Martin Luther King, Jr., who was slain over forty years ago. His assassin and the conspirators who were his accomplices thought that by silencing Martin's voice, they could kill his dream. Unfortunately, they were ill advised because it was too late to stop the momentum of Martin's dream. The combination of God's calling, a dream whose time had come, and Martin's masterful orations meant that the movement couldn't be minimized and forced the civil rights issue to the forefront of America's consciousness. Though it is debatable whether or not all of the aspects of Martin's dream have come to fruition, the dream itself finds a place in the hearts of all of those who love peace and strive to obtain social equality and justice.

Dreams and words are a powerful combination. Words are the conduits that connect dreams to action and reality. Though one can act out based simply upon their thoughts—like a schizophrenic entertaining auditory hallucinations—it's not the norm, particularly when you're dealing with the kingdom of God. In the kingdom, words have impact. Proverbs 18:21 says, "the tongue has the power of life and death." In the Gospels, Jesus proclaimed "A good man brings good things out of the good stored up in his heart, and an evil man brings evil things out of the evil stored up in his heart. For the mouth speaks what the heart is full of" (Luke 6:45). So, whatever desires or dreams are in one's heart, his actions and his words shall reveal it. Herein is the problem. Life and death are in the power of the tongue; therefore, you can speak life or death to a dream. A dream revealed to the wrong individuals can solicit words and actions that can destroy the dream. Therefore, another's words or your own words can be a dream killer.

BACK TO JOSEPH'S DREAM

Returning to the account of Joseph and his dream in Genesis, chapter 37, our text reads:

> Joseph had a dream, and when he told it to his brothers, they hated him all the more. He said to them, "Listen to this dream I had: We were binding sheaves of grain out in the field when suddenly my sheaf rose and stood upright, while your sheaves gathered around mine and bowed down to it." His brothers said to him, "Do you intend to reign over us? Will you actually rule us?" And they hated him all the more because of his dream and what he had said.
>
> Genesis 37:5-8

Joseph was Jacob's favorite son because he was the son of his old age. Because of this, Joseph's older brothers were jealous and hated him. Joseph knew this. However, trying to seek the approval of his older brothers, he thought that by sharing his dream, his brothers would be understanding and appreciative. Like Moses, he was wrong. Instead of invoking brotherly love, hearing the dream made them hate Joseph even more. Remarkably, the first negative reaction from his brothers failed to convince Joseph to keep his mouth closed. After having another dream, he tells that one too, but this time he includes his parents. The text reads:

> Then he had another dream, and he told it to his brothers. "Listen," he said, "I had another dream, and this time the sun and moon and eleven stars were bowing down to me." When he told his father as well as his brothers, his father rebuked him and said, "What is this dream you had? Will your mother and I and your brothers actually come and bow down to the ground before you?"

So Joseph went after his brothers and found them near Do-than. But they saw him in the distance, and before he reached them, they plotted to kill him. "Here comes that dreamer!" they said to each other. "Come now, let's kill him and throw him into one of these cisterns and say that a ferocious animal devoured him. Then we'll see what comes of his dreams."

Genesis 37:9-10, 17-20

From these passages, we see that Joseph continued to tell his dreams to the wrong individuals. However, this time they were not just a little annoyed, they wanted to kill him and his dreams. It can be argued that this was all a part of God's plan, because at the end of the story, Joseph declares, "You intended to harm me, but God intended it for good" (Genesis 50:20). However, our focus here is the practical application of the dangers of talking too much to the wrong people. The bottom line is that had Joseph kept his mouth shut; his brothers may have tolerated him, instead of wanting to kill him.

Many of the problems that we have in life come from us not being able to keep a lock on our mouths. Deep emotional wounds are caused from what people say to us, particularly when it comes to family members. However, we can be our own worst enemy by giving our detractors ammunition to shoot at us. Your haters are not interested in helping you become successful. There are endless stories of people's dreams never coming to past simply because they were discouraged by loved ones. You expect your enemies not to encourage you, but we become frazzled by people who are close to us when they blindside us with discouraging words. To discourage someone means to take out the courage from them. Too often, our words are killing instead of healing.

How many businesses were never started, or inventions were never developed, or books were never written, because a person with a dream told his dream to someone who discouraged them with words like, "Why do you want to start a business? Don't you know most business fail in their first five years?" Ironically, the person that is discouraging you has never had a regular job, let alone thought about owning their own business. This is why you must be wise in whom you share your heart's desires and dreams with, because people who are going nowhere love taking someone else with them. Don't kill your dream by telling it to the wrong person. Be prayerful and wise. Check yourself. Ask yourself, why am I feeling the need to tell this person my business in the first place? Is it going to further the cause? If not, then why do they need to know? We should keep our mouths closed, and lean not to our own understanding. Let God direct your paths. Opening your mouth at the wrong time, to the wrong people, is a definite dream killer.

EVIL IMAGINATIONS

One of the greatest struggles that we have to face as Christians is our own thought life. How we think can be the single greatest obstruction that blocks us from reaching our destiny. So many times, we default to blaming the devil for our troubles. However, often it's the enemy—within me—that's causing the problems. In Proverbs 23:7 we find these words, "For as he thinketh in his heart, so is he ..." (KJV). In other words, whatever dominates your thought life, that's what you invariably become. That's why it's so important to take charge of the places you allow your mind to go. The devil knows that if he can control your mind, he can change your destiny. Therefore, he puts much emphasis on inundating the masses with all sorts of evil communication specifically designed to corrupt good manners and intentions, by changing what you think about God, yourself, and your destiny.

In Proverbs 4:23 we are given this instruction, "Above all else, guard your heart, for everything you do flows from it." This verse begins with the phrase "above all else." In other words, the writer is saying the most important thing to consider is to guard your heart (heart is synonymous for mind). Every reason, every motive, every action, every plan, every agenda, every goal, every relationship, everything that you do, is a direct reflection of what's in your heart. For example, you don't accidentally curse anyone out. It was already in your heart. Your anger pushed foul language to the surface, and the expletives came out of your mouth. However, it's the devil's job to exacerbate what's already in you. He'll tempt you in an area where you already have a weakness, or an area where he already has developed a stronghold. This is why the phrase popularized by the late comedian Flip Wilson, "the devil made me do it," would never be a defense before God. You are responsible for what you do.

The Bible teaches that in the last days shall come perilous times, where crimes, violence, and murder will be unparalleled. This is particularly true here in America, where gun violence and mass shootings are off the charts. The interval between mass shootings seems to be shortening every year, with increasingly deadlier results. One of the most horrific cases of mass murder was Sandy Hook Elementary School in Newtown, Connecticut, where twenty-year-old Adam Lanza massacred twenty-five souls before taking his own life.

As America was stunned by this massacre, the investigation as to what motivated the young man to commit such a heinous act turned up that Adam played violent video games, and had been obsessed with watching footage of the Columbine Massacre and other mass murders. It is reported that Connecticut Senator Christopher Murphy stated, "Guns and video games played a role in the shootings." A renewed outcry against violent video games was heard throughout the nation. Graphic cases like this are the reason the Bible tells us "above all else guard your heart." Because what gets in through the five senses, particularly through the eyes and ears, can have a dramatic effect on what you do, where you go, and ultimately where you end up. Clearly, the violence in which Lanza internalized by way of the Internet and violent video games had a great influence on him acting out violently.

The phenomenon of people being influenced to act out on internalized mental imagery can also be seen with people who are addicted to drugs. For example, crack addicts will tell you that in between the times that they use, they're constantly thinking about that next hit. Images of past episodes play over and over in their mind until they can no longer resist the temptation to get high. Once they use again, those memories become the fresh impressions that play in their mind until they go on their next run. No matter how much education or socioeconomic status you have, none of that has anything to do with preventing addiction. Drugs are an equal opportunity destroyer. Doctors, lawyers, husbands, housewives, and even pastors have walked away from jobs, careers, family, and pulpits in order to pursue their addictions. These are all life-altering, destiny-destroying, dream-killing events from which some never return. Singlehandedly, evil imaginations have destroyed countless lives and derailed untold destinies. Now we can understand why the verse says, "Above all else, guard your heart, for everything you do flows from it." Evil imaginations are dream killers.

Filthy Dreamers

Just as there are people who have God-given dreams, there are also those who the enemy inspires to have evil dreams. In Jude 7-8, the Bible tells us about these people and characterizes them as filthy dreamers. Jude writes:

> Even as Sodom and Gomorrha, and the cities about them in like manner, giving themselves over to fornication, and going after strange flesh, are set forth for an example, suffering the vengeance of eternal fire. Likewise also these filthy dreamers defile the flesh, despise dominion, and speak evil of dignities. (KJV)

In this text, we see individuals who are given over to lust. They are lovers of pleasure more than lovers of God. They are the type that come to you and draw you with various enticements that appeal to the flesh. People like this always seek to detour or derail you from anything that's pure and holy. They say, "Let's go party," while you should be studying. Or, "Let's go out and eat," while you're fasting. Whatever it is that you're trying to accomplish, they always come to you with something opposite. All they think about is the lust of the flesh, the lust of the eye, and the pride of life. They can't rest at night unless they've corrupted somebody else. The whole goal of filthy dreamers is to draw you off of your purpose.

We must be vigilant not to let filthy dreamers infect our God-given dreams with their wickedness. You can never be so hungry for success that you're willing to compromise and sell out your dream by linking to the wrong individuals that end up taking you down. The dream that God gave you was to have good success, not wicked success. It was to make you rich and add no sorrow. Not rich and can't get to sleep at night and have no peace or joy. In your God-given dream, you were to be prosperous, successful, increasing, and abounding in every good work. However, if you become yoked with a filthy dreamer, your ways will be corrupted and your dream voided.

Recently, a popular weekly television show that highlights crime stories did a segment on two brilliant African American young women who were so smart that they received full-ride scholarships to Harvard University. Both young women had big dreams for their futures. As students in grade school and high school, they worked hard to maintain 4.0 GPAs and dreamed of one day being accepted into an Ivy League university. However, it wasn't until they reached the halls of Harvard that everything changed for the worse. One of the young women wasn't concerned with her syllabus, curriculum, or classes, but instead wanted to live life in the fast lane. She became attracted to a dropout drug dealer. Soon he had her selling drugs for him on the Harvard campus. She then befriended the other young woman who had earned a scholarship to Harvard, and brought her into the drug game too. As they became entrenched in the drug game, both of them plotted to steal some drugs from another dealer. In this rip-off, no one was supposed to get hurt. But the person who was robbed ended up being murdered.

When it was all over, one of the girls ended up going to prison for accessory after the fact and lying to the grand jury. The other woman wasn't imprisoned because she turned State's evidence; however, she was still convicted and thrown out of Harvard for dealing drugs.

How did all of this happen? Being hooked with a filthy dreamer. It wasn't enough for them to have a full scholarship to the most prestigious university in the country and practically being guaranteed a bright future after graduation. They forsook their own dreams, and became yoked to a filthy dreamer who enticed them to live life in the fast lane, chasing after the so-called "fast buck." In reality, the only thing that happened fast was murder, ruin, and prison time. Following the lead of a filthy dreamer is a certain dream killer.

What is it that we can learn from all this? All of us have an innate weakness. All of us are guilty of entertaining a sinful thought. All of us are subject to error in a moment of enticement. All of us can succumb to a desire to fulfill the lust of the flesh. However, the Bible tells us how to get the victory over the evil imaginations in the battlefield of our mind. In 2 Corinthians 10:3-5, we find this passage:

For though we walk in the flesh, we do not war after the flesh: (for the weapons of our warfare are not carnal, but mighty through God to the pulling down of strong holds;) Casting down imaginations, and every high thing that exalteth itself against the knowledge of God, and bringing into captivity every thought to the obedience of Christ. (KJV)

Here Paul informs us that in our warfare arsenal, we have supernatural weaponry to pull down what he identifies as strongholds. In order to defeat any enemy, we must become versed in their tactics and strategies, and understand exactly what is a stronghold. To do this, we must go to 1 Samuel 17:1-2, to see a stronghold in action. The text reads:

> Now the Philistines gathered their armies together to battle, and were gathered at Sochoh, which belongs to Judah; they encamped between Sochoh and Azekah, in Ephes Dammim. And Saul and the men of Israel were gathered together, and they encamped in the Valley of Elah, and drew up in battle array against the Philistines. (NKJV)

From this passage, we get an idea of what a stronghold really is. The Philistines had set up camp at Sokoh, which was a territory that belonged to Judah. The first thing that we see here is that the Philistines were in possession of seized territory. This is how a stronghold begins, from territory that is either yielded to or taken by the enemy. Secondly, once the territory is seized, the enemy sets up camp and entrenches its forces. Thirdly, once they have dug in, they harass, intimidate, and launch attacks. Therefore, the purpose of an enemy stronghold is to seize more of the opposition's ground until their opponent is either destroyed or forced to retreat and abandon all their territory.

However, in 2 Corinthians 10, Paul isn't concerning himself with a natural stronghold nor a physical enemy because he states outright that the weapons in this warfare are not carnal or physical. They're not of this world, but they're mighty through God to the pulling down of strongholds. They're not by human power nor by human might, but by His Spirit. Secondly, Paul isn't dealing with a conflict on a terra firma battlefield, as was the case with Israel and the Philistines. Instead, this battlefield is in our minds, where our "imaginations" and "thoughts" are used by the enemy as weapons against us. The enemy knows the power behind imaginations and thoughts. He knows that if he can possess your mind, he has your body too. He knows that if he can inject enough fear and doubt and degrade and devalue your faith, it will be impossible for you to please God. However, we do have weapons to defeat the attacks from the enemy. In Ephesians 6:12-18, Paul lists what weapons we have in our arsenal.

> For our struggle is not against flesh and blood, but against the rulers, against the authorities, against the powers of this dark world and against the spiritual forces of evil in the heavenly realms. Therefore put on the full armor of God, so that when the day of evil comes, you may be able to stand your ground, and after you have done everything, to stand. Stand firm then, with the belt of truth buckled around your waist, with the breastplate of righteousness in place, and with your feet fitted with the readiness that comes from the gospel of peace. In addition to all this, take up the shield of faith, with which you can extinguish all the flaming arrows of the evil one. Take the helmet of salvation and the sword of the Spirit, which is the word of God. And pray in the Spirit on all occasions with all kinds of prayers and requests. With this in mind, be alert and always keep on praying for all the Lord's people.

In this passage, we see that God has equipped us to battle a wicked, demonic enemy. Against an enemy like this, assault rifles and tanks are useless. God has designed specific weapons for the Christian to use in his fight against the strategies of the devil. These weapons are mighty through God and specifically designed for destroying enemy strongholds. However, we're warned that we must put on the "full" armor of God in order to be able to "stand your ground." In the kingdom of God, "stand your ground" is a good law, because we cannot be giving up any ground to the enemy.

The first weapon is the "belt of truth." In chapter 3, we examined how the truth is greater than facts. The truth sets you free and incorporates every aspect. Facts are limited to what's known and only focuses on the particulars. When you know the truth, you can't be incarcerated by a lie. Jesus said, "My word is truth." This is why an active study life and attending weekly Bible study is so vital to a child of God. It's not just information you're getting; it's a weapon you're going to need when the enemy attacks.

The second weapon is "the breastplate of righteousness." Knowing that you are in right-standing with God is vital for the Christian. In Revelation 12:10, Satan is called "the accuser of our brothers and sisters." The devil will always bring accusation against us to God, and try to make us feel guilty and unworthy because we all have fallen short. However, the Bible says that "God made him who had no sin to be sin for us, so that in him we might become the righteousness of God" (2 Corinthians 5:21). In Christ Jesus, all of our sins have been forgiven. Through faith, righteousness is imputed (placed) on our account. The enemy wants us to get distracted with the darts of accusation he shoots at us. But we need not worry about his arrows because they can't penetrate the breastplate of righteousness.

The third weapon in our arsenal is having our "feet fitted with the gospel of peace." This is an offensive weapon because you're ready and equipped to share the Gospel message with all those who are seeking God. Paul quoting Isaiah 52:7 in Romans 10:15 said, "How beautiful are the feet of them that preach the gospel of peace, and bring glad tidings of good things!" We are ever ready to present Christ to everyone and prepared to give a response for the hope that dwells in us. In this dying world, people are searching for the light of hope that only the Gospel message can bring. Every time the light of the glorious gospel shines in this dark world, people are translated out of the kingdom of darkness and into the Kingdom of His dear Son. Sharing the Gospel with someone is a direct blow against the kingdom of darkness.

The fourth weapon is the "shield of faith." Faith is in direct opposition to fear and is a crucial weapon in our arsenal. In 1 John 5:4 we find these encouraging words, "For everyone born of God overcomes the world. This is the victory that has overcome the world, even our faith." Of all the many purposes that our faith serves, the warfare aspect of our faith is victory over the world, and more specifically, the god of this world, Satan. Our faith has a great effect on how we think, and the enemy knows that. If the devil can interject fear and doubt into your mind about God's promises to and for you, he knows that he can short-circuit your dreams with thoughts and imaginations that exalt themselves against the knowledge of God. Satan is always trying to challenge what God has said, as he did to Eve in the Garden when he said, "hath God said?" However, because we have the shield of faith to stop those attacks, we are sure to be overcomers.

The fifth weapon in our arsenal is the "helmet of salvation." Although helmets are designed to protect your head, cranial protection is not the focus here. The helmet of salvation protects us from attacks in our thought life that come to contradict the veracity and efficacy of Christ's finished work at Calvary. Salvation implies deliverance from every wicked thing that comes to steal, kill, and destroy. Salvation also means that we are the children of God, and have been bought with a price, redeemed by the blood of the Lamb, and sealed until the day of redemption. The helmet of salvation is critical in protecting us from all of the competing religious and secular philosophies in the world, and all of the other voices of false witnesses that come to militate against our position in Christ. This is why Jesus said, "My sheep listen to my voice; I know them, and they follow me. I give them eternal life, and they shall never perish; no one will snatch them out of my hand" (John 10:27-28). The helmet of salvation protects you from doubting "who you are," and "whose you are."

The sixth and final weapon in our arsenal is the "sword of the spirit," which is the Word of God. The best example of using the Word of God as a weapon against a satanic attack

is found in the Luke, chapter 4 concerning Christ's temptation in the wilderness. Satan hurled three temptations at Jesus,
and the Lord defeated him each time, but not with any fan-
tastic displays of power, like calling fire down from heaven or
summoning angelic assistance. Jesus countered each of Satan's
temptations with simple yet powerful responses. He would say
"It is written," and respond with an appropriate scripture each
time. The truth is that God's Word accomplishes that which he
has purposed it to do, and it shall not return unto him void.
It is life-giving, powerful, cannot be undone or broken, and is
eternal. As a weapon of our warfare, in God's Word we have the
mind of Christ. His wisdom and power are at our disposal. The
Word is life, light, and power that the devil cannot defeat, and
he knows it. The only place that he can really challenge God's
Word is on the battlefield of our mind.

In addition to the weapons of our warfare, in Philippians
4:8, we also are given some very practical things that we can
do to keep these evil imaginations and thoughts from exalting
themselves against the knowledge of God and corrupting our
God-given imaginations and dreams. The passage reads:

> Finally, brethren, whatsoever things are true, whatsoever things
> are honest, whatsoever things are just, whatsoever things are
> pure, whatsoever things are lovely, whatsoever things are of good
> report; if there be any virtue, and if there be any praise, think on
> these things. (KJV)

This passage teaches that we do have control over our thought
life. We're told to "think on these things." In other words, we

don't have to dwell on thoughts and imaginations that exalt themselves against the knowledge of God. The knowledge of God obviously means the written Word of God, but it also means the words that God has spoken to you about His purpose for your life. Your God-given imaginations and dreams are the stuff that "Big Ideas" are made of.

Nine
RECOVERING THE LOST DREAM

The United States continues to be in the grips of a lethargic economic recovery from a recession that was touted as the worst economic downturn since the Great Depression of the 1930s. Millions of hardworking Americans lost jobs as both large and small business alike were forced to downsize and/or went belly-up and closed their doors for good. Economists were saying that the entire economy was on the verge of collapse if they allowed companies that were so-called "to big too fail" to go under. Therefore, Congress voted to enact a multi-trillion-dollar bailout package. The largest financial institutions and multinational insurance companies received a safety net to prevent them from going into an abysmal economic free-fall.

During this same time that Wall Street was being bailed out, the people on "our streets" were left to fend for themselves. As jobs were lost, bills and mortgages were not being paid. That set off a chain reaction that caused families, businesses, and municipalities to go bankrupt. Foreclosures shot up to the highest number in history as property values sunk underwater, and millions of Americans watched all of their net worth dwindle away. As a result, many hard working middle class people, for the first time in their lives, found themselves in food lines, and even worse, homeless. People lost jobs, homes, businesses, careers, retirement accounts, investments, and most of all their dreams.

The question that's before us now is what do you do when that which has taken you a lifetime to accumulate is gone in a matter of a few months? How do you maintain your sanity, integrity, and most of all your relationship with God? In times like these, how do you handle the depression when for the first time in your life you don't have any answers or options? No one is bailing you out. But hold on; don't tie that hangman's noose yet. The only one who is truly "too big to fail" has promised to supply all of your needs according to His riches in glory. In this final chapter on "Recovering the Lost Dream," the life of King David gives us some biblical perspective and answers on all these pressing issues.

DAVID'S DREAM BEGINS

David was anointed to be the second king of Israel after Saul's failed administration was coming to an end. While David was out tending sheep, God sent the prophet Samuel to anoint and appoint David as King Saul's successor. From that point on, David dreamed of what it would be like to be the king. I'm sure that he imagined himself as sitting on the throne in the palace and ruling this great nation. I'm sure that David saw himself directing the affairs of the nation. He probably imagined himself leading the Lord's army in battle and winning victories over Israel's enemies. No doubt, David dreamed of Israel having peace and prosperity under his leadership. Yes, I'm sure that David arranged a picturesque dreamscape full of honor and splendor as he imagined himself as being king. However, David soon found out that the paths to our dreams are not paved in gold, and life throws unexpected obstructions and roadblocks at us along the way.

By this time, David had already slain Goliath and was the champion of Saul's army. People were already touting David as a better leader than Saul. Their mantra was, "Saul has killed his thousands, but David killed his ten-thousands." This aggravated Saul so greatly that an evil spirit would come upon him and cause him to want to kill David. After Saul had made several attempts on his life, David was forced to flee. During about a ten-year period, David went through a number of difficult circumstances and hardships as he wandered in the wilderness with a band of rag-tag outcasts who became his mighty men of valor.

For more than a decade, David must have felt year after year that his dream and his reality would never intersect. Samuel said he would be king, but where was the glory of the promised kingdom?

How do you handle it when your dream and reality are incongruent? Have you ever been under so much pressure that you begin to question the validity of your dream? How did the vicissitudes of life turn your dream into a nightmare of circumstances? Has your imagination misled you and now has you wandering down the wrong path? How is it that you're stuck in the wilderness when God has called you to be a winner? Where has your dream gone?

As we continue our examination of David's life, we find one unlikely partnership that placed David in a very precarious situation. David ends up joining with Israel's archenemy, the Philistines, to go to war against Saul. David was about to attack the very nation over which he was destined to be king. Have you ever been in a situation where you're doing something to destroy your own destiny? The wrong relationship, the wrong partnership, the wrong relocation, the wrong career path. Sometimes our bad decisions can make us our own worst enemy. David's disdain for Saul made him lose sight of his dream to be king. David was only interested in payback, even if it meant fighting alongside the same nation that produced Goliath. What David needed was some divine intervention to fix his focus. In 1 Samuel 29, let's examine what happened that changed David's misguided course.

> As the Philistine rulers marched with their units of hundreds and thousands, David and his men were marching at the rear with Achish. The commanders of the Philistines asked, "What about these Hebrews?" Achish replied, "Is this not David, who was an officer of Saul king of Israel? He has already been with me for over a year, and from the day he left Saul until now, I have found no fault in him." But the Philistine commanders were angry with Achish and said, "Send the man back, that he

may return to the place you assigned him. He must not go with us into battle, or he will turn against us during the fighting. "But what have I done?" asked David. "What have you found against your servant from the day I came to you until now? Why can't I go and fight against the enemies of my lord the king?" Verses 2-4, 8

Here we see how the tide of events turned David from participating in a military campaign against his own nation. He was ordered to return to Ziklag, where he had set up camp for all his men, their wives, children, and all of their possessions.

Before David could return to Ziklag, some Amalekite raiders burned their homes and took all of their wives, children and possessions. The Bible records for us the anger and lamenting that David and his men experienced when they returned to Ziklag. The Bible says that they wept until they could weep no longer. From there, things got worse because an insurrection was at hand. David's men talked of stoning him. However, instead of coming unglued, here is what David did.

> And David was greatly distressed; for the people spake of stoning him, because the soul of all the people was grieved, every man for his sons and for his daughters: but David encouraged himself in the LORD his God. And David said to Abiathar the priest, Ahimelech's son, I pray thee, bring me hither the ephod. And Abiathar brought thither the ephod to David. And David enquired at the LORD, saying, Shall I pursue after this troop? shall I overtake them? And he answered him, Pursue: for thou shalt surely overtake them, and without fail recover all.
>
> 1 Samuel 30:6-8 (KJV)

Even in the midst of hellish circumstances, David did what you and I must do to recover our lost dreams. First David encouraged himself in the Lord. Many of you have suffered losses during the years of this brutal recession. You lost jobs, homes, savings, investments, and retirement portfolios. Additionally, it seemed like everyone around had given up on you and even kicked you to the curb. Your "supposed to be" friends all turned their backs on you, and some of your family members did even worse.

On the other hand, maybe your losses were not the result of a bad economy but they stemmed from bad decisions that either you or someone else made. No matter what caused the losses, if you can just encourage yourself in the Lord, He will fight your battles for you. You encourage yourself by recounting all of the times God saved you and brought you out. You have to remember what the Word of God says: that no weapon formed against you shall prosper, and if God delivered you before, He will do it again.

After David had encouraged himself in God, he took the next step, and he called for the priest to bring him the ephod. The ephod was a garment that was worn by priests as they went into the sanctuary to minister before the Lord. David was saying, "I have to step into my priestly office and go in before the Lord to get some divine direction on what to do." Today, we must do the same thing. In 1 Peter 2:9, the Word God tells us "…you are a chosen people, a royal priesthood, a holy nation, God's special possession, that you may declare the praises of him who called you out of darkness into his wonderful light." Through Christ Jesus, our great High Priest, we're a chosen generation of priests, that we should declare the praises of our

God. Today we don't need an ephod because we are already clothed with a garment of praise and filled with the Holy Spirit. We also have the right to come boldly before the Throne of Grace to obtain mercy and help in a time of need.

So once David went in before God's presence, he asked the Lord, "Shall I go recover our stuff?" The Lord said, "Go get 'em. The victory is already yours, and you shall recover all your stuff and theirs too."

During these uncertain perilous times, just like David, many of you have lost the "substance" of your dreams. You may have lost your dream job to downsizing. You may have lost your dream home to foreclosure. Yes, you may have also lost your dream car to repossession. And many of you lost the hope of seeing a brighter day. It might be a struggle just to sleep at night because worrying about all your problems has made you lose your joy. However, if you can just put on your spiritual ephod, get to the church, make your way to the altar, and get in the presence of God, He will release you to go and get the stuff that the enemy stole from you. Tell the devil, "I want my stuff back!"

By the time David returned to Ziklag from recovering their possessions and loved ones, the battle between the Philistines and King Saul was already over. Unfortunately, the battle was a great loss for Israel. Saul and his sons were all killed, including David's best friend, Jonathan. After a while of fasting and mourning in Ziklag, David once again inquired of the Lord whether or not he should go back to any of the cities of Judah. And the Lord told him, "Yes, go back." However, David had no idea which city to go back to, so he asked the Lord. The Lord responded, "Hebron."

I'm sure David's imagination was running wild as to what he would face in Hebron. Maybe after so many years, his dream to be king was on the back burner—or off the stove completely! Maybe his heart was still broken over the loss of his friend, Jonathan, and the national loss to the Philistines. Maybe the Philistines laid in wait for David when he returned. He didn't know what to expect. All he knew was where God told him to go. However, soon after David arrived in Hebron, the elders of Judah met him and anointed him to be the king. At the age of thirty, David stepped into the purpose that had dominated his imagination and dreams ever since he was a teenager.

The Lost Dream

The issue of recovering a lost dream is somewhat of a misnomer, because the question is, is a dream ever really lost? Like files on a computer that have been deleted, you may not have access to them, but are they really deleted? The answer is no; they're still there. Only the extension for the file has been deleted, but the information is still there. The issue is access. It's like a day when the skies are filled with dark clouds, we say that the sun is not out. But in reality, the sun is shining just as bright as it always has, but to see it you must be above those clouds. Often when it comes to our lost dreams, life's issues, like the clouds, can obstruct our perspective and block access to recalling our dreams.

Remember, your God-given dreams are given to you to fulfill your purpose. Even if you are having difficulty recovering the dream, it's still valid. For example, when King Nebuchadnezzar forgot his dream that within itself didn't diminish the veracity of the dream. It was still valid. Even after Joseph was thrown in a pit and locked in a prison, his dream was still valid. Even though he thought he might never see Jacob or his brothers again, the dream was still valid. Whatever calling, whatever gift, whatever desire God gave to you, it's still there. It's not lost in the sense of no longer being in existence. It's only lost because you're not accessing it. Maybe because of some new circumstances in life, you no longer believe that the dream can come true. Maybe you've been convinced that it wasn't a God-given dream. Maybe it has been such a long time coming, that you have given up on its fulfillment. Whatever the case, all God has to do is give you a moment of clarity and it will put you back on the road to see the dream once again.

As we discovered in chapter 5, everyone dreams, and most of us have between five and seven dreams per night. However, many of us think that we don't dream at all because we don't remember our dreams. Dreams are like vapors that dissipate quickly when we awake. We're unable to recall some of our dreams while others remain active in our memories for years. Many theories have floated around for years about our inability to recall dreams. Freudian theories say these are repressed thoughts and wishes that aren't important enough to remember. Another theory says that other thoughts simply get in the way. However, when it comes to God-given dreams, whenever the children of God cannot recall or access their God-given dreams, somehow, some way the problem could be the enemy or the problem may lie within us.

THE EXCELLENT SPIRIT

Two of the key elements in receiving anything from God are expectation and faith. Ask yourself, what am I believing and expecting God to do in my life. This book is all about igniting your expectations to actualize and/or recover your lost dreams. One of the ways we can understand the characteristics of an effective dreamer is to look at the life of one of the greatest prophetic dreamers of all time, Daniel. Daniel 5:12 gives us insight into the personality and character traits of a dynamic dreamer. Our text reads:

> Forasmuch as an excellent spirit, and knowledge, and under-standing, interpreting of dreams, and shewing of hard sentenc-es, and dissolving of doubts, were found in the same Daniel, whom the king named Belteshazzar: now let Daniel be called, and he will shew the interpretation. (KJV)

What immediately jumps out in this text is that Daniel is said to have had an "excellent spirit." *The American Heritage Dictionary* defines *excellent* as being: "of the highest or finest quality; exceptionally good of its kind." In the Bible, the Hebrew word *yattir* means "exceedingly excellent." In other words, Daniel possessed a dynamic personality that, among other things, was kind, engaging, intellectual, considerate of others, and wise. Some of his character traits would have been; integrity, loy-alty, trustworthiness, faithfulness, consistency, and grateful-ness. A person who possesses these traits has an excellent spirit.

Have you ever been around someone that puts you at ease

and is a joy to be around? They have an aura about themselves that draws you in, and you can tell right away that there's something special about them. That was Daniel.

In the first chapter of Daniel, we learn how he became involved in the Babylonian administration. In verses 3-4 and 6, the text reads:

> ...to bring into the king's service some of the Israelites from the royal family and the nobility—young men without any physical defect, handsome, showing aptitude for every kind of learning, well informed, quick to understand, and qualified to serve in the king's palace. Among those who were chosen were some from Judah: Daniel, Hananiah, Mishael and Azariah.

As we see from this text, Daniel and the three Hebrew boys stood out from the very beginning. They were smart, good-looking, healthy, and had a good attitude and aptitude to match. They were the type of people that any corporation would love to hire. To describe them in today's vernacular, these boys "had it going on." However, though all of these traits are great, they don't get you anywhere with a God, who is not a respecter of persons. For Daniel to have a truly "excellent spirit," he had to have a close relationship with God. That's what truly made him excellent.

In Daniel 1:8, we see that from the very beginning, Daniel had purposed in his heart to live a sanctified (separated for God) life. "But Daniel resolved not to defile himself with the royal food and wine, and he asked the chief official for permission not to defile himself this way." This may seem to be insignificant, but it's huge. Think about it. Daniel was a slave, who had found the favor to serve in the king's court. But not only that, he had the privilege to eat the king's food—the best food—and to drink the king's wine, the finest wine. Most people then and even today would see that as "favor," particularly under adverse conditions such as slavery. Daniel's fellow slaves who didn't serve in the king's court may have been starving and would have eaten anything you put in front of them whether it was kosher or not.

Surely, Daniel could reason, "God would understand it if we skipped the dietary restrictions under the Mosaic Law in conditions of captivity." Even Jesus spoke of David eating the priest's bread, which was unlawful, when he was hungry (Mark 2:24-27). However, Daniel didn't concern himself with that. He purposed in his own heart not to defile himself with the royal food, even though an acceptable circumstance to excuse dietary restrictions under the law existed. That's faithfulness! That's integrity! As a result of Daniel and the three Hebrew boys being so steadfast in their walk with the Lord, the king declared that they were ten times better than his magicians and astrologers.

After consulting with the king, Daniel makes some very important statements regarding his abilities. Daniel says:

> No wise man, enchanter, magician or diviner can explain to the king the mystery he has asked about, but there is a God in heaven who reveals mysteries." [Then Daniel says:] " As for me, this mystery has been revealed to me, not because I have greater wisdom than anyone else alive, but so that Your Majesty may know the interpretation...."
>
> Daniel 2: 27-28, 30

In these passages, Daniel is quick to acknowledge that it is not about him, but it's all about God. He also states that the purpose of the dream is that "you may know the interpretation."

God does not give us dreams so that they can be forgotten. I believe the disconnect between receiving and remembering our dreams is all in the way we think. In the battlefield of our minds, we must learn to pull down strongholds that come to contradict the Word of God in our heart. This is why having an excellent spirit is also vital. People who put God first learn to act on God's directions whether He speaks to their heart or to them in a dream. God has given you a dream to know it. The fact that we cannot recover our dreams suggests that we should make some adjustments in our life while seeking God for direction.

To get more insight on this subject let's examine Paul's passionate plea to believers in Romans 12:1-2.

> And so, dear brothers and sisters, I plead with you to give your bodies to God because of all he has done for you. Let them be a living and holy sacrifice—the kind he will find acceptable. This is truly the way to worship him. Don't copy the behavior and customs of this world, but let God transform you into a new person by changing the way you think. Then you will learn to know God's will for you, which is good and pleasing and perfect. (NLT)

In these two verses, Paul pleads with us to give our bodies to God, considering all that He has done for us. Essentially this means we should have an attitude of gratitude and be willing to live a sacrificial life unto God. As the refrain from the Gospel hymn says, "Jesus paid it all. All to him I owe." God wants us to live a sanctified life like Daniel did, separated unto Himself, away from the corrupting influences of the world. That's what is acceptable to Him. The greatest act of worship is not clapping your hands or stomping your feet, speaking in tongues, yelling hallelujah or cutting a step. The greatest act of spiritual worship is to present yourself unto God—holy and acceptable.

In the first part of verse 2, Paul instructs us "not to copy the behavior and customs of this world...." We live in a dark and evil society where God has commissioned the saints to be the light. As we let our light shine, we glorify God and draw those around us to Christ. However, in the second part of the verse, the apostle says, "Let God transform you into a new person by changing the way you think. Then you will learn to know God's will for you, which is good and pleasing and perfect." This is an awesome truth. God transforms us by changing the way we think. So we will "learn to know" God's good, pleasing and perfect will for our life. We will learn to know what He has called us to do. We will learn to know our gifts. We will learn to know our purpose in life. We will learn to know His voice. And we will learn to know His dreams and how to recover the ones that are lost.

5-STEPS TO RECOVERING YOURS DREAMS

Here are five simple things that you can do that will help you recover your dreams. Step 1, each night before you go to sleep, lay your hands on your head and give God permission to invade your sleep. I know some of you may think this is a crazy idea, but if you can have faith that's crazy enough to believe that the Word of God is true, then you can "acknowledge him in all yours ways, and He will direct thy paths."

Step 2, is to pray and ask Him to touch your mind in a deep cerebral way, to give you dreams that will be a forecast of your future. In faith and expectation, ask God to give you clear dreams, with a matching soundtrack, so you will not only see, but you will also be able to hear God's call and plan for your life. Ask God to show you in dreams those who should not be in your life, all the smiling-face haters who are positioning themselves between you and your destiny. Ask God to expose the traps that were set against you so you will know how to move in and out among all the people around you. Ask him to reveal why you had to go through some stuff in your life that you did and how it helped shape and preserve you for where you are today. Ask God to give you a glimpse of your child's or family's future. Ask Him to show you how to operate in your gift full-time.

Step 3, is to write the dream and make it plain. In Habakkuk 2:2 NKJV the Lord gives this instruction, "…Write the vision And make it plain on tablets, That he may run who reads it." The instruction is simple, if you want to remember your dreams, "Write them down." There is a 40-day *Dream Journal* found on pages 143-181. Have a pen and this book ready on your nightstand. As soon as you wake up, write down what you dreamed about. As you continue journaling, you'll start seeing the dream themes that God is revealing to you.

Step 4, is after you have written down your dreams, pray that God is going to make whatever you've been dreaming come to pass. Then engage your imagination to expect to see these dreams fulfilled. Pray twice a day for dreams to come true.

Step 5, is to read the Word of God. Each morning after journaling and prayer, start reading Psalm 119. It's the longest chapter in the Bible, and every verse is about the Word of God. Pray that God will germinate the seed of the Word in your life and bring forth God-given dreams and big ideas according to His will. Remember, it is God who already knows the plans that He has for you, to prosper you and bring you to an expected end. The Holy Spirit and the Word are in perfect agreement, and it's the Holy Spirit's job to bring all things back to your remembrance.

GIMMIE BACK MY STUFF!

Finally, the last aspect of recovering the lost dream is recovering the substance of our dreams. In chapter 5, we discussed the pouring out of the Holy Spirit on the Day of Pentecost. The verses Peter quoted were taken from the book of Joel. In the same book, God also speaks of great restoration. In Joel 2:24-26 the Bible says:

> The threshing floors will be filled with grain; the vats will overflow with new wine and oil. "I will repay you for the years the locusts have eaten—the great locust and the young locust, the other locusts and the locust swarm—my great army that I sent among you. You will have plenty to eat, until you are full, and you will praise the name of the LORD your God, who has worked wonders for you; never again will my people be shamed.

At the beginning of this chapter, we talked about the Great Recession that is the worst economic recession since the Great

Depression, which was triggered by the subprime mortgage crisis. This recession was so widespread that it devastated economies all over the world. It was during this time that millions of Americans suffered devastating economic losses in the wake of business, banks, mortgage lenders, real estate companies, insurance companies, city and state municipalities, even the federal government, collapsing or being on the brink of collapsing. With the economy in a full nosedive, the middle class was practically wiped out. Like a plague of locusts, unforgiving economic times devoured millions of hard working people's dreams when they lost their homes, jobs, businesses, savings, investments, college funds, retirement funds, and anything else that contributed to their net worth. It was all gone. What was left was a spirit of despondency, desperation, depression and desolation.

However, in Joel 2, Judah, a nation built on agriculture economy, didn't face a subprime mortgage crisis. But they faced a plague of locusts which, after destroying all of the vegetation, would leave not only economic collapse but famine, starvation, disease, and death in their wake. As bad as this circumstance seemed, God promised to restore everything that the plague of locusts destroyed.

Though many of you have suffered unparalleled economic lost where the things of your dreams were destroyed during the recession, God will restore everything that the economic locusts have devoured. Homes will be restored. Jobs will be restored. Businesses will be restored. Savings will be restored. Investments will be restored. College funds will be restored.

Retirement funds will be restored. Health, hope, and relationships will all be restored. Truly, every one of your heart's desires will be restored. God is going to supply all your needs and the desires of your heart. He will restore everything the devil stole from you. So don't give up hope, don't give in. Don't take down. Your Father in heaven is the author and finisher of your faith, and he most certainly is too big to fail. Truly, in these last days, God has poured out His Spirit upon all flesh. God has big ideas for all of those with God-given dreams. Go forth and fulfill the dreams that God has given you. Be confident that he that began a good work in you, will carry it on to completion until the day of Christ Jesus. May the Lord continue to richly bless you, in Jesus's mighty name.

The End

40-Day Dream Journal

The Significance of the Number 40

The number 40 figures prominently throughout the Scriptures. It is often related to vigil, fasting, mourning, repentance and punishment. Biblical events such as the number of days the flood lasted, the age Moses was when he responded to the call to be the deliverer, the number of years he spent in Midian, and the number of years the Israelites wandered in the wilderness were all 40. Goliath challenged and defied Israel for 40 days. David and Solomon both reigned as king for 40 years. Jonah preached in Nineveh for 40 days, and Jesus fasted for 40 days in the wilderness. However, most importantly, for 40 days after his resurrection, Jesus taught and prepared His disciples for the manifestation of a new spiritual organism called the "Church." To sum it up, 40-days is a preparatory period—the start of a long journey—for God to unveil His plans for your life that often comes through dreams.

The Importance of Journaling

Writing down your thoughts and ideas is a technique that many successful people employ on a regular basis. With all of the circumstances that we are confronted with daily, it is easy to forget to do something that previously crossed your mind. Therefore, writing down important thoughts is an indispensable tool that will help you chart a course to your destiny. As we have learned throughout this book, God often speaks to us through our dreams. This is why writing them down is so important so you won't forget what your God-given dreams were about.

This *40-Day Dream Journal* will assist in this process. After you wake up in the morning, quickly write down your dreams before they are forgotten. Be careful to follow the "5-Steps to Recovering Your Dreams" found on pages 136-138.

Finally, each journal dream day has one inspirational passage of scripture taken from the longest chapter in the Bible, Psalm 119. As I mentioned in Step 5, all of the verses in this chapter teach about the importance of God's Word in the life of a believer. Jesus said, my Word is truth...and the truth shall make you free—free to unlock the unfolding revelation of your destiny often contained within the context your dreams.

Date_____

Blessed are those whose ways are blameless, who walk
according to the law of the LORD.

Psalm 119:1

Dream Content: _____

_____

_____

_____

_____

_____

_____

_____

_____

_____

_____

_____

_____

_____

_____

_____

_____

_____

_____

_____

_____

_____

_____

Date_____

Blessed are those who keep his statutes and seek him with all
their heart— they do no wrong but follow his ways.

Psalm 119:2-3

Dream Content: _____

_____

_____

_____

_____

_____

_____

_____

_____

_____

_____

_____

_____

_____

_____

_____

_____

_____

_____

_____

_____

Date_____

You have laid down precepts that are to be fully obeyed.

Psalm 119:4

Dream Content: _____

_____

_____

_____

_____

_____

_____

_____

_____

_____

_____

_____

_____

_____

_____

_____

_____

_____

_____

_____

_____

_____

_____

_____

_____

Date_____

Oh, that my ways were steadfast

in obeying your decrees!

Psalm 119:5

Dream Content: _____

_____

_____

_____

_____

_____

_____

_____

_____

_____

_____

_____

_____

_____

_____

_____

_____

_____

_____

_____

_____

_____

_____

Date_____

Then I would not be put to shame
when I consider all your commands.

Psalm 119:6

Dream Content: _____

_____
_____
_____
_____
_____
_____
_____
_____
_____
_____
_____
_____
_____
_____
_____
_____
_____
_____
_____
_____
_____
_____
_____
_____

Date_____

I will praise you with an upright heart

as I learn your righteous laws.

Psalm 119:7

Dream Content: _____

_____

_____

_____

_____

_____

_____

_____

_____

_____

_____

_____

_____

_____

_____

_____

_____

_____

_____

_____

_____

_____

_____

_____

Date_____

I will obey your decrees;

do not utterly forsake me.

Psalm 119:8

Dream Content: _____

_____

_____

_____

_____

_____

_____

_____

_____

_____

_____

_____

_____

_____

_____

_____

_____

_____

_____

_____

_____

_____

_____

_____

Date_____

How can a young person stay on the path of purity?

By living according to your word.

Psalm 119:9

Dream Content: _____

_____

_____

_____

_____

_____

_____

_____

_____

_____

_____

_____

_____

_____

_____

_____

_____

_____

_____

_____

_____

_____

_____

_____

Date_____

I seek you with all my heart;

do not let me stray from your commands.

Psalm 119:10

Dream Content: _____

_____

_____

_____

_____

_____

_____

_____

_____

_____

_____

_____

_____

_____

_____

_____

_____

_____

_____

_____

_____

_____

_____

_____

Date_____

I have hidden your word in my heart

that I might not sin against you.

Psalm 119:11

Dream Content: _____

_____

_____

_____

_____

_____

_____

_____

_____

_____

_____

_____

_____

_____

_____

_____

_____

_____

_____

_____

_____

_____

_____

_____

_____

Date_____

Dream Content: _____

_____

_____

_____

_____

_____

_____

_____

_____

_____

_____

_____

_____

_____

_____

_____

_____

_____

_____

_____

_____

_____

_____

_____

_____

Date_____

With my lips I recount

all the laws that come from your mouth.

Psalm 119:13

Dream Content: _____

_____

_____

_____

_____

_____

_____

_____

_____

_____

_____

_____

_____

_____

_____

_____

_____

_____

_____

_____

_____

_____

_____

Date_____

I rejoice in following your statutes

as one rejoices in great riches.

Psalm 119:14

Dream Content: _____

_____

_____

_____

_____

_____

_____

_____

_____

_____

_____

_____

_____

_____

_____

_____

_____

_____

_____

_____

_____

_____

Date_____

I meditate on your precepts
and consider your ways.
Psalm 119:15

Dream Content: _____

_____

_____

_____

_____

_____

_____

_____

_____

_____

_____

_____

_____

_____

_____

_____

_____

_____

_____

_____

_____

_____

_____

_____

Date_____

I delight in your decrees;

I will not neglect your word.

Psalm 119:16

Dream Content: _____

_____

_____

_____

_____

_____

_____

_____

_____

_____

_____

_____

_____

_____

_____

_____

_____

_____

_____

_____

_____

_____

_____

_____

_____

Date_____

Be good to your servant while I live,

that I may obey your word.

Psalm 119:17

Dream Content: _____

_____

_____

_____

_____

_____

_____

_____

_____

_____

_____

_____

_____

_____

_____

_____

_____

_____

_____

_____

_____

_____

_____

Date_____

Open my eyes that I may see
wonderful things in your law.
Psalm 119:18

Dream Content: _____

_____

_____

_____

_____

_____

_____

_____

_____

_____

_____

_____

_____

_____

_____

_____

_____

_____

_____

_____

_____

_____

_____

_____

_____

Date_____

I am a stranger on earth;

do not hide your commands from me.

Psalm 119:19

Dream Content: _____

_____

_____

_____

_____

_____

_____

_____

_____

_____

_____

_____

_____

_____

_____

_____

_____

_____

_____

_____

_____

_____

_____

_____

Date_____

My soul is consumed with longing

for your laws at all times.

Psalm 119:20

Dream Content: _____

_____

_____

_____

_____

_____

_____

_____

_____

_____

_____

_____

_____

_____

_____

_____

_____

_____

_____

_____

_____

_____

_____

_____

Date_____

You rebuke the arrogant, who are accursed,

those who stray from your commands.

Psalm 119:21

Dream Content: _____

_____

_____

_____

_____

_____

_____

_____

_____

_____

_____

_____

_____

_____

_____

_____

_____

_____

_____

_____

_____

_____

_____

Date_____

Remove from me their scorn and contempt,

for I keep your statutes.

Psalm 119:22

Dream Content: _____

_____

_____

_____

_____

_____

_____

_____

_____

_____

_____

_____

_____

_____

_____

_____

_____

_____

_____

_____

_____

_____

Date_____

Though rulers sit together and slander me,

your servant will meditate on your decrees.

Psalm 119:23

Dream Content: _____

_____

_____

_____

_____

_____

_____

_____

_____

_____

_____

_____

_____

_____

_____

_____

_____

_____

_____

_____

_____

_____

_____

_____

_____

Date_____

Your statutes are my delight;

they are my counselors.

Psalm 119:24

Dream Content: _____

_____

_____

_____

_____

_____

_____

_____

_____

_____

_____

_____

_____

_____

_____

_____

_____

_____

_____

_____

_____

_____

_____

_____

_____

_____

_____

Date_____

I am laid low in the dust;

preserve my life according to your word.

Psalm 119:25

Dream Content: _____

_____

_____

_____

_____

_____

_____

_____

_____

_____

_____

_____

_____

_____

_____

_____

_____

_____

_____

_____

_____

_____

_____

_____

Date_____

I gave an account of my ways and you answered me;

teach me your decrees.

Psalm 119:26

Dream Content: _____

_____

_____

_____

_____

_____

_____

_____

_____

_____

_____

_____

_____

_____

_____

_____

_____

_____

_____

_____

_____

_____

Date_____

Cause me to understand the way of your precepts,

that I may meditate on your wonderful deeds.

Psalm 119:27

Dream Content: _____

_____

_____

_____

_____

_____

_____

_____

_____

_____

_____

_____

_____

_____

_____

_____

_____

_____

_____

_____

_____

_____

Date_____

My soul is weary with sorrow;

strengthen me according to your word.

Psalm 119:28

Dream Content: _____

_____

_____

_____

_____

_____

_____

_____

_____

_____

_____

_____

_____

_____

_____

_____

_____

_____

_____

_____

_____

_____

_____

_____

_____

Date_____

Keep me from deceitful ways;

be gracious to me and teach me your law.

Psalm 119:29

Dream Content: _____

_____

_____

_____

_____

_____

_____

_____

_____

_____

_____

_____

_____

_____

_____

_____

_____

_____

_____

_____

_____

_____

_____

Date_____

I have chosen the way of faithfulness;

I have set my heart on your laws.

Psalm 119:30

Dream Content: _____

_____

_____

_____

_____

_____

_____

_____

_____

_____

_____

_____

_____

_____

_____

_____

_____

_____

_____

_____

_____

_____

_____

_____

Date_____

I hold fast to your statutes, LORD;

do not let me be put to shame.

Psalm 119:31

Dream Content: _____

_____

_____

_____

_____

_____

_____

_____

_____

_____

_____

_____

_____

_____

_____

_____

_____

_____

_____

_____

_____

_____

_____

_____

Date_____

I run in the path of your commands,

for you have broadened my understanding.

Psalm 119:32

Dream Content: _____

_____

_____

_____

_____

_____

_____

_____

_____

_____

_____

_____

_____

_____

_____

_____

_____

_____

_____

_____

_____

_____

_____

_____

Date_____

Teach me, LORD, the way of your decrees,

that I may follow it to the end.

Psalm 119:33

Dream Content: _____

_____

_____

_____

_____

_____

_____

_____

_____

_____

_____

_____

_____

_____

_____

_____

_____

_____

_____

_____

_____

_____

_____

Date_____

Give me understanding, so that I may keep your law

and obey it with all my heart.

Psalm 119:34

Dream Content: _____

_____

_____

_____

_____

_____

_____

_____

_____

_____

_____

_____

_____

_____

_____

_____

_____

_____

_____

_____

_____

_____

_____

Date_____

Direct me in the path of your commands,

for there I find delight.

Psalm 119:35

Dream Content: _____

_____

_____

_____

_____

_____

_____

_____

_____

_____

_____

_____

_____

_____

_____

_____

_____

_____

_____

_____

_____

_____

_____

_____

Date_____

Turn my heart toward your statutes

and not toward selfish gain.

Psalm 119:36

Dream Content: _____

_____

_____

_____

_____

_____

_____

_____

_____

_____

_____

_____

_____

_____

_____

_____

_____

_____

_____

_____

_____

_____

Date_____

Turn my eyes away from worthless things;

preserve my life according to your word.

Psalm 119:37

Dream Content: _____

_____

_____

_____

_____

_____

_____

_____

_____

_____

_____

_____

_____

_____

_____

_____

_____

_____

_____

_____

_____

_____

_____

_____

_____

Date_____

Fulfill your promise to your servant,

so that you may be feared.

Psalm 119:38

Dream Content: _____

_____

_____

_____

_____

_____

_____

_____

_____

_____

_____

_____

_____

_____

_____

_____

_____

_____

_____

_____

_____

_____

Date_____

Take away the disgrace I dread,

for your laws are good.

Psalm 119:39

Dream Content: _____

_____

_____

_____

_____

_____

_____

_____

_____

_____

_____

_____

_____

_____

_____

_____

_____

_____

_____

_____

_____

_____

_____

_____

Date_____

How I long for your precepts!

In your righteousness preserve my life.

Psalm 119:40

Dream Content: _____

_____

_____

_____

_____

_____

_____

_____

_____

_____

_____

_____

_____

_____

_____

_____

_____

_____

_____

_____

_____

_____

Connect With Us:

Jamal Bryant Ministries

www.jamalbryant.org

Empowerment Temple
Baltimore, Maryland

www.empowermenttemple.org

https://twitter.com/jamalhbryant

https://www.facebook.com/jamalbryant

About the Publisher

Let us bring your story to life! With Life to Legacy, we offer the following publishing services: manuscript development, editing, transcription services, ghostwriting, cover design, copyright services, ISBN assignment, worldwide distribution, and eBook production and distribution.

Throughout the entire production process, you maintain control over your project. We also specialize in family history books, so you can leave a written legacy for your children, grandchildren, and others. You put your story in our hands, and we'll bring it to literary life! We have several publishing packages to meet all your publishing needs.

Call us at: 877-267-7477, or you can also send e-mail to: Life2Legacybooks@att.net. Please visit our Web site:

www.Life2Legacy.com

CPSIA information can be obtained at www.ICGtesting.com
Printed in the USA
BVOW07s0805141114

375058BV00001B/1/P